Journal Your Way

"Rain! O Glorious rain! ...

Director got upset (because) ...

Home at 6:00 ...

home about five ...

COOL AND CRISP DAY • BUSY AT WORK, AS USUAL

(CHINESE) • CALLED ABOUT ROLLEIFLEX TLR ...

HIGH— OFFERED $200 ~ WE'LL SEE • HANNA: WENT ...

ITCHEN, BATHROOMS • 30 MINUTES ON NORDIC TRA...

UP EARLY (5:30AM) — WILL AND I WENT TO GA...

ATE NICE B'FAST IN SHELBY— NPR TALKING...

FFICIALLY PRESIDENT OF ADMIN. MGT DIVISION ...

TCHED "THE KLUTZ- NUTTY PROFESSOR II" • SU...

Up about 9, coffee - Max Parton Sr. and Jr. arrived ...

Done about 2 • Duke smoked Michigan, Kentucky ...

ur of Homes with Trudy and Ross - groceries. ...

lower basement • Ben studying - then gone about ...

Up @ 9am, Pancakes for ...

Long overdue! - Ben over ...

will back and forth, in and out ...

made omelette's for ...

COLD IN A.M., BUT VERY PLEASANT ...

LUNCH AT RIO BRAVO WITH MISSUS ...

R. ANNARINO, RETIRING FOL...

AME, HOWEVER ... WHO'S WHO OF ...

Better weather today drove MGB to work ...

out of Police "MEG" program - will be controversial • ...

her for insignificant reasons - jeez • Home about ...

Doc Chey's • Missus shopped • Will motivated, signed up ...

MISSUS IN HOSPITAL • GOT TO ST. JOSEPH'S ...

BY 10:30! • MISSUS SORE AND TIRED (CAN'T REST IN ...

Journal Your Way

Designing & Using Handmade Books

Gwen Diehn

LARK CRAFTS

Asheville

LARK CRAFTS

An Imprint of Sterling Publishing
387 Park Avenue South
New York, NY 10016

Previously published as Live & Learn: Real Life Journals:
Designing & Using Handmade Books

First Paperback Edition 2013
Text and Illustrations © 2010 by Gwen Diehn
Photography © 2010 by Lark Crafts, an Imprint of Sterling Publishing Co., Inc.

ISBN 978-1-60059-492-2 (hardcover) 978-1-4547-0411-9 (paperback)

Library of Congress Cataloging-in-Publication Data

Diehn, Gwen, 1943-
  [Real life journals]
  Journal your way : designing & using handmade books / Gwen Diehn.
      pages cm
  Previously published: Real life journals : Desigining & using handmade books / Gwen
Diehn, in the series Live & learn.
  Includes index.
  ISBN 978-1-4547-0411-9
  1. Bookbinding--Amateurs' manuals. 2. Scrapbook journaling. I. Title.
  Z271.D54 2013
  686.3--dc23
                                    2012042569

Distributed in Canada by Sterling Publishing
c/o Canadian Manda Group, 165 Dufferin Street
Toronto, Ontario, Canada M6K 3H6
Distributed in the United Kingdom by GMC Distribution Services
Castle Place, 166 High Street, Lewes, East Sussex, England BN7 1XU
Distributed in Australia by Capricorn Link (Australia) Pty. Ltd.
P.O. Box 704, Windsor, NSW 2756, Australia

For information about custom editions, special sales, and premium and
corporate purchases, please contact Sterling Special Sales at 800-805-5489
or specialsales@sterlingpublishing.com.

Email academic@larkbooks.com for information about desk and examination copies.
The complete policy can be found at larkcrafts.com.

Manufactured in China

2 4 6 8 10 9 7 5 3 1

larkcrafts.com

Editor: Deborah Morgenthal

Assistant Editor: Mark Bloom

Art Director: Dana Irwin

Art Production: Shannon Yokeley

Illustrator: Gwen Diehn

Photographer: Stewart O'Shields

Cover Designer: Celia Naranjo

For Marjorie Dittmann Smith

CONTENTS

two very different reds...
the barberry and the
tulip poplar - no yet fresh
and dried... two stages of the
game.

a walk before
the holidays and so
time for a detail... the
overall after the new year
trying to see the greater
whole and time has
taken the smooth red
surfaces for herself

Choose Your Own Bookbinding Adventure
foldout chart inside front cover

Bookbinding Essentials
foldout chart inside back cover

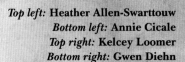

Top left: **Heather Allen-Swarttouw**
Bottom left: **Annie Cicale**
Top right: **Kelcey Loomer**
Bottom right: **Gwen Diehn**

Introduction

We all reach a point in our lives when we realize that we know better than anyone else just what we need and want. It's a fine place to be, after years of being told by others what to buy, what to eat, how to dress, how to be healthy, and even—of all things—what type of blank book to use for a journal.

As a long-time lover of journals and journaling, I have several bookshelves devoted to my journals. It's easy to see which are the real life ones: like the Velveteen Rabbit, they're more than a bit worn and clearly well loved. A few have sprung bindings; others are over-stuffed with memorabilia—notes, ticket stubs, boarding passes, and postcards from friends. Among these full and lively journals stand a few almost-empty ones. In spite of their bright and beautiful covers, they didn't work out, and I abandoned them quickly. This book is about what you can do to be sure that *all* of your journals are real life journals that can enrich and deepen the very reason you chose to keep a journal in the first place.

Years ago one of my sons gave me a little journal wrapped in buttery leather. It fit my hand like a chunky bar of soap. I loved everything about it: the paper that was the color of apricot mousse and thick enough to take watercolor washes as well as crisp pen lines; the wrap-around cover that concealed a tiny envelope and had a tail that could tie up the book along with a pen and a small map—a tidy package that easily slipped into my jacket pocket.

I quickly filled the journal with sketches and notes, and I decided to make a similar book because I wasn't able to find one like it where I lived. But I wanted to fiddle with the design a little to better suit my needs. The new journal I made had more pages so that I wouldn't use it up so quickly. This small change made the journal even better. This was my first experience of designing from the inside out, and I was hooked.

When you design from the inside out, the result is driven by a personal, specific purpose. In this case, the processes or activities you want the journal to document or reflect are the drivers of the design. After all, only you can know how you want to use your journal and what you want it to do for you. And that is how this book came to be. I know that the journals I design and make for myself for a particular purpose are the ones I yearn to hold and love to fill, journals that become a home away from home.

In *Real Life Journals* you'll learn to:

Determine the type of journal that will best fit your particular, possibly exotic or loopy, project or activity.

Create a design that will yield the perfect journal for what you want at this time.

Choose the materials and book forms based on your unique design.

Build the journal using your design.

Use your journal in ways that deepen, broaden, and enhance your activities, projects, travels, and relationships.

Chapter One, Design Inventory, consists of a list of easy questions for you to answer that will help you figure out how your journal can fulfill your journaling "purpose." For example, if you're traveling and want the book to be portable, you may want it to fit in your pocket and have a cover that can withstand being taken in and out of that pocket. If you want to use paints in your journal, at least some of the pages will need to be heavy enough to withstand being wet.

GWEN DIEHN *Italy Journal*, 2006
6 x 7 x 1 inches (15.2 x 17.8 x 2.5 cm); Sewn on Tapes binding laced into a flexible paper cover; commercial rubber letter stamps, pen, watercolor

Choose Your Own Bookbinding Adventure

When you finish answering these questions, you'll have a design inventory for the journal you want. Then you'll be ready to turn to the foldout chart stored in the envelope inside the front cover. Like the popular interactive children's book series, *Choose Your Own Bookbinding Adventure* puts you in charge of the outcome of your journal-designing "story." Using the information in your design inventory, you'll answer another series of questions that will point you to instructions for making one of 16 types of books—the one that will best suit your individual needs.

Personal Journals
Chapter Two explores how this experience of designing from the inside out worked for nine people who helped me test-drive the design inventory and the *Choose Your Own Bookbinding Adventure* foldout. Based on their answers, I made a custom journal for each of them. After a few months, I talked to them to find out how their journals were working. You'll learn about the projects, practices, and other occasions that instigated their own designs and journal keeping. You'll come to understand how they chose their particular journal design, see pages from their journals, and probably get ideas for your own book.

The Basics
In Chapter Three, you'll find information about bookbinding materials, tools, and techniques. There's also information on what I call "page building," by which I mean the many ways you can add visual entries to your journal pages.

Bookbinding Essentials
To make life a little easier, there's a handy foldout called Bookbinding Essentials stored in an envelope inside the book's back cover. This reference guide details the techniques you'll use no matter which book form or cover you choose to make. Keep it open on your worktable, and refer to it as needed.

The Instructions
When you come to the end of *Choose Your Own Bookbinding Adventure*, you'll be directed to one of the book forms in Chapter Four; and the book form directions will help you choose one of the cover forms in Chapter Five. Detailed instructions and illustrations in these chapters will help you make your own custom journal.

Inspiration
Journal keeping has a rich and often surprising history. In Chapter Six, you'll learn about the unusual, persistent, and creative practices of keepers of journals, daybooks, notebooks, commonplace books, and other record books in myriad cultures, past and present.

Your Turn
If you've ever sewn your own clothing, baked an apple pie, or built a backyard tree house, you know the satisfaction of doing it yourself. When you also design it yourself, you take control of the project from its inception. You use the accumulated knowledge and wisdom of years of experience to design from the inside out. You'll be amazed at the results. Let's get started!

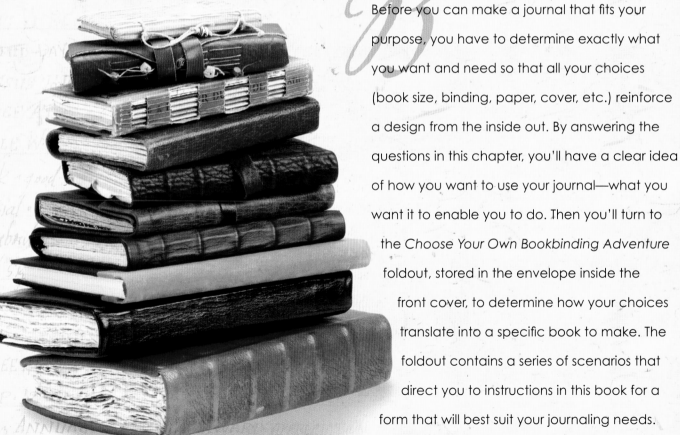

design inventory

Before you can make a journal that fits your purpose, you have to determine exactly what you want and need so that all your choices (book size, binding, paper, cover, etc.) reinforce a design from the inside out. By answering the questions in this chapter, you'll have a clear idea of how you want to use your journal—what you want it to enable you to do. Then you'll turn to the *Choose Your Own Bookbinding Adventure* foldout, stored in the envelope inside the front cover, to determine how your choices translate into a specific book to make. The foldout contains a series of scenarios that direct you to instructions in this book for a form that will best suit your journaling needs.

Design Inventory

Grab pen and paper, and write down your answers to these questions.

Imagine that you're immersed in your project (or travels or activity, etc.) and you're ready to make an entry in your journal.

WHERE ARE YOU? Inside your house curled up with the cat? Pulling weeds in the community garden? Strapped to the mast of a sailboat in a storm? Think about the many places where you might be making entries in this particular journal.

WHAT KINDS OF ENTRIES ARE YOU MAKING IN THE BOOK? Are you writing, sketching, pasting in flat things, mapping, collecting seeds or shells, making a chart, drawing a plot plan, planning, or reviewing Chinese verbs? What else?

Now envision the book after a month's use. What has the book helped you do? For example, has it helped you focus, make decisions, see better, remember more, figure out or plan something?

OF WHAT USE IS THE BOOK TO YOU *NOW*, AFTER YOU'VE BEEN USING IT FOR A WHILE? Can you use it as a reference book, a collection of ideas for future projects, or an aid to memory? How else can you use it?

The Binding

The way in which the book is sewn or glued together makes some activities possible while restricting or even prohibiting others.

WHEN YOU IMAGINE YOURSELF USING THE BOOK, WHAT SHOULD THE BINDING ALLOW YOU TO DO? Consider if any of these features would be useful for this book.

Would you like the book to open flat and stay open by itself?

Could you fold pages back on themselves like a waiter's order book or a reporter's notebook?

Could you add extra pages or other flat elements?

Could you easily remove or replace the pages (if this is something you want to be able to do)?

Would you like the book to be a double book, one that opens from two places, such as the front as well as the back, or on two sides of the cover?

Should the book have double-folded pages into which you could slip single, smaller pages or flat items?

Should it include pockets or envelopes?

Should it have a secret compartment somewhere, a place in which to slip something you want to keep hidden?

What else might the binding do or allow for?

The Cover

All covers protect the text blocks they enclose to some degree. They also contribute to the aesthetics of the book, as well as affect how easy it is to use and handle. Some covers reflect certain types of content; others offer inspiration; still others set up false expectations that actually heighten the impact of the contents by the tension thus created. For example, a plain black business-like cloth cover with a tight cord wrapping might open onto a wonderful surprise of fold-out pages bursting with color and wild handwriting—plans for a festival, or designs for stage sets, or a collection of old family recipes.

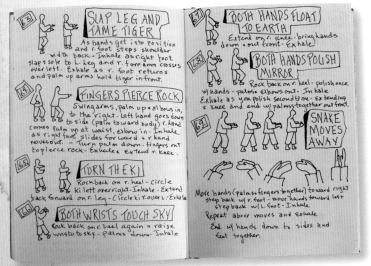

SANDY WEBSTER *T'ai Chi Journal*, 2005
6 x 8 inches (15.2 x 20.3 cm); hand-bound book; pen PHOTO BY ARTIST

What do you want the cover to do or enable you to do? Consider all that apply.

🐛 Should it to protect the pages from dirt, water, rain, grease, or the strain and stress of being placed in dirty places from time to time?

🐛 Should it let you roll up the book and slip it into your pocket or backpack or bag?

🐛 Should the cover incorporate artwork or significant material, such as an encrustation of local soils, beach sand, seeds, or a collage of drawings?

🐛 Should it protect the pages from dust while it stands on a bookshelf?

🐛 Would you like it to look elegant and traditional?

🐛 Do you want it to incorporate a wrap-around flap that can carry pens or pencils?

🐛 Would you like the cover to have windows into which you can slip photographs, drawings, or other flat things?

🐛 Is there anything else you want the cover to do?

Size of the Book

When you open the book past the first page, you'll see a two-page spread.

🐛 What size should each single page be?

🐛 Do you need some larger, foldout pages? What size and about how many?

🐛 Do you need some smaller pages that can serve as stubs or anchors for envelopes or other flat elements? What size and how many?

🐛 What size should the closed book be?

🐛 Approximately how many pages/how thick should the book be?

Paper Choices

Consider carefully what you want the journal's paper to make possible. Different types of paper work better with different mediums.

What do you want to do that a specific type of paper would enable you to do better?

Consider all that apply.

🐛 Draw plans, maps, and plot plans?

🐛 Write or sketch in pen?

🐛 Write or sketch in pencil?

🐛 Paint in watercolor or acrylic?

🐛 Paste on or collage paper elements such as photographs, ticket stubs, and other ephemera?

🐛 Write, draw, or paint on both sides of the sheet?

🐛 Trace things?

🐛 See through one page to the page underneath?

🐛 Reflect particular content (such as wrapping paper or maps that you have collected in your travels, or photocopies of letters from a friend)?

🐛 Is there anything else you want the paper to do?

Special Features

What other features would be nice to have in your journal? For instance, would you like:

🐛 A piggyback pamphlet book that you can slip into a pocket in the larger journal and take out when only a small book will do?

🐛 A place to carry writing and drawing equipment?

🐛 Pages that have been prepared with poured acrylic paint, coffee, tea, blobs of watercolors, or stamped textures?

🐛 Any other special features?

SARAH A. BOURNE *Scoville Journal Page*, 2004
7½ x 11½ inches (19 x 29.2 cm); hand-bound journal, magazine cut-out, typewriter PHOTO BY ARTIST

CHAPTER 2

personal journals

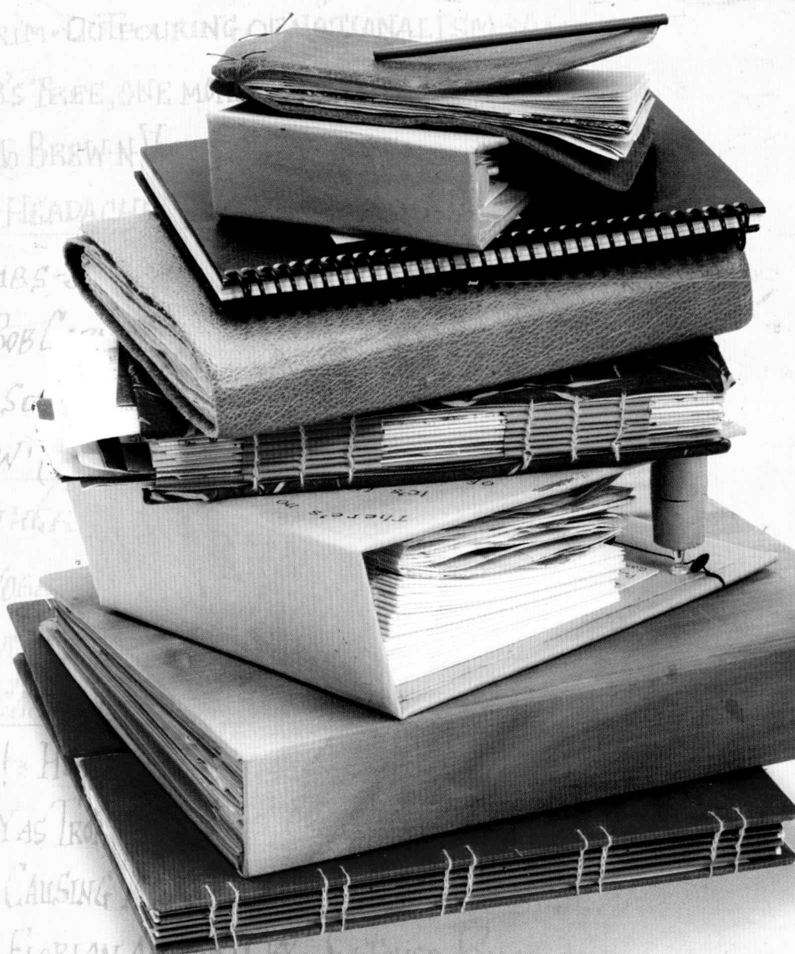

I invited nine people (including a father/daughter pair and a grandmother and her five little grandsons) to choose a kind of journaling activity that appealed to them, such as recording a trip, being involved with a practice, chronicling a project, learning something new, commenting about an experience or relationship, and being part of a group. Each person answered the questions in the Design Inventory and the *Choose Your Own Bookbinding Adventure* foldout. This process led to particular book forms and covers that I made for them. They used the journals for three months, and then I talked to them about their journaling experiences. In this chapter, the nine journal keepers reflect on their experiences using their real life journals.

Travel Journal

for Brigid Burns

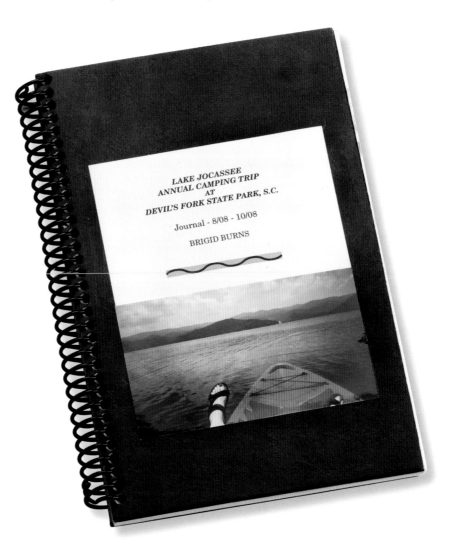

LAKE JOCASSEE
ANNUAL CAMPING TRIP
AT
DEVIL'S FORK STATE PARK, S.C.

Journal - 8/08 - 10/08

BRIGID BURNS

View from favorite swimming spot - the point near tent camping.

Establishing a beach head - floaties & sun shade Marietta & Constance & others.

Design Inventory

Brigid Burns is an established journal keeper, especially of travel journals. When I asked her what kind of custom travel journal she'd like me to make for her, she had very specific ideas. In the past, she'd been able to find readymade blank books of the perfect size, shape, and color. She'd even found some with a lined paper that she particularly liked. Unfortunately, the paper wasn't the best for the watercolor and acrylic paint that Brigid sometimes used. She wanted her custom journal to have paper that would stand up to watercolor and collage, as well as to pen and pencil drawing. The paper needed to be heavy enough to withstand writing and painting on both sides of the page. She also wanted each page to have lines on the bottom half, with empty space along the outside edge for comments. Finding lined paper that would suit her purposes was going to be the main challenge for this journal design.

Brigid told me that she wanted a spiral-bound journal that would stay flat when it was open. She intended to store her pen in the space created by the binding. She said the ideal size would be about 5½ x 8½ inches (14 x 21.6 cm) so that she could slip it in and out of her backpack or bag when traveling. She requested a stiff cardboard cover in a dark color.

She was very clear about the last design element. She didn't want an elaborate book that called attention to itself. "Unobtrusive" was the word she used, because she didn't want to be noticed when using the book. Also, overly crafted blank books intimidated her.

Food + Beverage - the other main activity - done on a lottery system this time (same as tent sites)

- 1st night's dinner: Warren & Joyce + Constance & Peter hosted
  - Bruschetta + drinks
  - Seafood salad (shrimp, scallops and ORZO)
  - Caesar salad, bread
  - Mojito pie - à la Warren
  - Coffee

- 2nd night's dinner: Marietta + Richard + Martin + Jean hosted
  - Roasted red pepper hummus, olive tapenade, crackers + drinks
  - Poulet Nicoise (stew with dried/cured black olives, tomatoes + yellow squash over couscous)
  - Salad + Ciabatta bread
  - Nanaimo Bars

Choose Your Own Bookbinding Adventure

Even though Brigid already had a clear picture of the book she wanted me to make for her, we decided to work through the Adventure process to help refine it even further.

In section A, Brigid chose a book that could fold over on itself, so she went to section B.

Her section B choice was for a book that would open wide and stay flat. That led her to section D.

In section D, Brigid chose *not* to replace every page, so we turned to section G.

Brigid didn't think she would need to add any flat elements to her journal, so we next went to section O.

Section O asked if she needed to bind in single sheets of paper, and she said yes, which led us to section P.

Section P suggested a Spiral binding … just what she wanted!

The next choice was paper type. Magnani Velata (page 51) seemed a good option, as it's a versatile paper, heavy enough to allow for writing on both sides of the page. The 120-pound weight would still keep the 30- to 40-page book relatively slender, which Brigid wanted. Since Velata is an unlined paper, I modified a purchased rubber stamp so that I could stamp lines on the paper in exactly the way she wanted—on the bottom half of all the sheets. Even though she hadn't specified a pocket, I added one to the inside cover at the back of the book.

For the covers, I used a piece of dark blue mat board. In order to make them slightly heavier, I laminated two boards together using YES paste (page 52) to make each cover.

Insights Gained

Brigid used her new journal during a weekend camping trip to a lake she has visited for many summers. She made journal entries, took photographs to add to the journal, and made some sketches and finished drawings. When we talked about her experience using the book, Brigid said that its design had definitely deepened the activity of journaling about a specific trip: "The journal grew beyond just [recording] the experience of what happened on our camping trip, per se, to gathering information about the history of the place when I returned home. I was excited to write down my findings, and my book grew to around 33 pages."

The best feature of the journal turned out to be the division of the page. She used the unlined top half for sketching, drawing, and adding photos, and the lined bottom half for writing. "The design gave me a sense of visual order. This didn't mean that I always obeyed the dictates of the layout, however; sometimes I wrote on the top and sides and drew on the bottom."

Did the Form Work?

Brigid said she was surprised at how interested she became in finding out about the lake and the state park in which it was located. She found herself recording "the many layers of (known) history that preceded us and the extent of flora and fauna in the park. This was my fourth visit to the lake—both camping and kayaking—and I never had that depth of curiosity before." Brigid said that after the camping trip, she contacted the park's information center to ask questions about the area's history, and based on what she learned, she went online to continue her investigation. As a result of her findings, she said, she'll return to the park at different times of the year, not just in the summer.

"I can honestly say that this journal-keeping project sharpened my attention, not only to the experience of camping, but to the history of the lake itself. I usually keep a journal while traveling, a hodge-podge of experiences and laundry lists of hotels, restaurants, and places, but never [anything] this focused. Now I have what amounts to a little story, and when I return to the journal, my memories of the trip are enriched."

The only modification she would make to this custom book was that next time she'd choose to work a little larger, with paper that had a little more grab for watercolors. Otherwise, she said her book worked fine.

> " The journal gave me a place to go that was always good, but [that] required letting go of judgment. "

Practice Journal

for Rebecca Blass-Casey

Rebecca Blass-Casey is a long-time personal journal keeper who wanted to see what would happen if she kept one journal to include both her meditation practice and her relatively new watercolor painting practice. Rebecca believed that her tendency to be critical of herself was inhibiting her painting. Not long ago, she had taken some watercolor painting classes in which technical skills were emphasized, and she felt unable to consistently paint the way the teacher suggested. She was discouraged about painting and sad that what had started out to be something she did for pleasure was turning into yet another occasion for self-criticism.

Recently, Rebecca had completed one painting that had seemed to flow out of her as if by magic, and she was pleased with it. But she said that she feared such magic could not happen again "when my mind is chattering away about some anxiety that I am not good enough." She hoped that the journal itself could prompt her to meditate, and that in the resulting calm state, she might be able to paint more freely on the journal page. She thought this approach could help her develop her own painting vocabulary, instead of just following someone else's rules.

One meditation practice that had helped quiet her mind in the past was to add a bead to a string of beads every time a thought intruded while she was meditating. Rebecca had noticed from day to day how the beads diminished in number as she became more focused. She therefore hoped to minimize her judgmental commentary during painting by moving beads along a string that could be attached to the journal.

Design Inventory

She wanted the journal to be small, with pages approximately 4 x 6 inches (10.2 x 15.2 cm), and to contain good quality watercolor paper. She thought 60 pages would be the right amount of paper, so she could try out the book for two months, doing a painting a day. She intended to paint on one side of each page, in case she decided to remove a painting from the book to frame it. Rebecca conceived of the journal as a small shrine-like object that would help focus her intention and calm her mind. She wanted the cover to be beautiful and even inspiring, perhaps incorporating a copy of the recent successful watercolor she had done, along with a line from a song she had written many years ago that described working when in flow.

Choose Your Own Bookbinding Adventure

Here's how things worked out for Rebecca when she went through the Adventure process:

🖎 Answering the question in section A, Rebecca said that since she would be doing most of her painting while sitting down at a table, her book would not need to have pages that would fold all the way over to the back. So we went to section C.

🖎 In section C, she chose a book that would open and stay flat. She then turned to section H.

🖎 The question in section H about being able to potentially remove and replace every page interested Rebecca, as she could imagine wanting to take out finished pieces and replace them with more paper, so she then turned to section J.

🖎 Section J suggested a Flat-Style Australian Reversed Piano Hinge binding. The directions for that binding style said it would work with a hard cover, which Rebecca thought would make the book more shrine-like and sturdy.

Because Rebecca wanted the pages to be oriented in horizontal or "landscape" format, we decided to bind the book so that it opened from bottom to top instead of side to side. The hinge area of the binding would provide a small space on which Rebecca could make notes, such as the number of beads used that day. In order to facilitate opening the book completely and turning the relatively heavy pages over out of the way, we decided to attach the text block to the back cover only. The text block was so thick, with 60 pages of heavy watercolor paper, that it seemed a good idea to make little columns out of old corks and two pushpins to support the cover boards when the book was closed. The edge of the cover could rest on the columns, and the string of beads would fit nicely between the columns.

We made a color copy of Rebecca's favorite "in-flow" painting at a size that would fit in a window in the cover. (See page 56 for directions on how to make a window in a covered board cover.) We then used purchased rubber stamp letters and a stamp pad to print the words of the song on the cover.

Insights Gained

After two months of keeping the journal, Rebecca said, "The design of the book, beginning with my 'magic' painting and meditational song, lent itself to encouragement that I could do this. I never would have painted this many watercolors up to this point. My lifelong problem has always been discipline and stick-to-it-iveness. So bringing an enjoyable meditational practice into my life is a good thing."

I asked her if there had been any surprises as she kept the journal. She said that, even though her intention was to let go of criticism and judgment, she still found herself critical, until one day, late in the two months, something happened. "The final ugly straw was when I did a value study and [then] painted a horse in front [of it]. It was so poorly done… As I began to pull a bead for this dark thought, I realized that here was a test to see if I could rise above my judgment and love *what is*. I decided not to pull a bead. On that picture I wrote 'Loving What Is.'"

Rebecca said the project made her realize that *doing* a painting is more important than *thinking* about it. "I had a clearer understanding of how it felt to be focused. No anxiety. It became easier to get to that state. Being present in the moment and loving *what is* were breakthroughs in my thinking. [I] better understood [it]

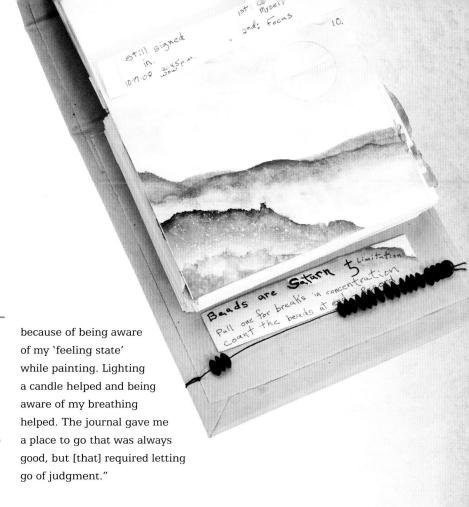

because of being aware of my 'feeling state' while painting. Lighting a candle helped and being aware of my breathing helped. The journal gave me a place to go that was always good, but [that] required letting go of judgment."

Did the Form Work?

Rebecca could already imagine the ways she would modify the book when she made it herself. She liked the inspiration the book offered, and said that every time she got the journal off the shelf, she would look at the cover and remember there was a time when she was "in the flow." But she would have liked fewer pages—60 pages ended up feeling daunting—and she thought she might experiment with a smaller overall size for the book cover, in order to make it more portable and easier to take to other locations. She would also choose a different brand of watercolor paper because she realized she prefers a less textured paper. Changing the paper is a very easy thing to do when you design and make your own journal.

Project Book
for Jane Gale McSpadden

Jane McSpadden had recently purchased a new digital camera and was shooting a lot of pictures. She decided to take a photograph of the same subject every day until she had 100 photographs, and then she'd move on to a different subject. She began by photographing trees. She was taking notes about light conditions and camera settings in a little spiral notebook. When I invited her to be a participant in *Real Life Journals*, she expressed an interest in finding out what direction her current project might take if she used a notebook that would enable her to include prints of her photographs along with the statistics, in addition to other kinds of notes.

Design Inventory

Jane envisioned using this notebook out in the field, so it needed to be small enough to slide in and out of her bag. It also needed to be easy to hold and make notes in while standing up and leaning against her car. She began to think a little more broadly about the kinds of entries she might make, and decided she wanted the pages to be slightly larger than she was accustomed to using and of heavier, lined paper.

Jane also wanted some means of attaching printouts of her photos as an alternative to pasting her photos directly to the page.

Finally, she greatly loved the feel of a soft leather cover and thought that this material would not only feel good but would be durable enough to protect the pages inside.

Choose Your Own Bookbinding Adventure

Here's what we learned working through the Adventure questions.

Jane needed a book that was flexible enough to allow her to fold the cover and the pages around to the back, so she turned to section B.

She didn't need the book to open and stay flat, but said that she always worked in it while holding it open, often leaning against her car. So she then went to section E.

In section E, she learned that a Ledger binding with a flexible cover would work well for her. When we looked at directions for making a Ledger, we noticed that it would be a simple matter to add stubs to the binding so that it would be easy to add elements such as printouts of her photographs.

The notebook I made for Jane (see below) is 4 x 6 inches (10.2 x 15.2 cm), with a soft leather cover that flops back easily. At first we thought it would need a rubber band to hold the flopped-over pages and cover, but that proved unnecessary. I stiffened up the back cover by laminating a piece of heavy paper to it, making it better for serving as a writing surface. I used 120 lb. Velata for the pages and stamped lines on the bottom half of each page using a modified purchased rubber stamp.

Insights Gained

After using her book for a few weeks, Jane especially liked how convenient it was for writing in. She believed the design had helped her expand the scope of relevant data that she could record about the subject she's photographing. In addition, the layout greatly facilitated organizing the data: "It heightened my awareness when I was out in the field of good opportunities of things to photograph. It sensitized my eye."

The best feature turned out to be the leather cover, because when Jane opened the notebook, it stayed open and in place on the roof of her car: "This made it very easy for me to be immediate, which is important, because if I trust things to memory I don't get the details."

Did the Form Work?

Jane said the stubs were so useful that she glued in some extras. When she makes another book herself, she plans to bind in more stubs—one per page. She'd also make the stubs longer than one inch because she wrote down more information than she expected. Jane liked the lined paper, but when she makes her own notebook, she'll modify the stamp to have more widely spaced lines to better accommodate her handwriting. She felt that the paper itself was inviting and a pleasure to write on.

Jane pasted photos onto some of the stubs and folded the extra-long printouts so that they would fit into the book. She began making sketches and taking notes about photography and about a museum exhibition she saw. Toward the end of the book, her increasingly lovely photographs punctuated sections of notes that added context to her work, as well as technical references.

"I became more consistent," Jane said, "It amped my excitement about the photography project. I became more careful. One picture (the baby tree—at left) happened because I told myself it was going in my journal. I checked the light quality several different times during the day to make sure the one I chose was exactly right. I wanted it to be an expressive picture of this tree we had just planted to replace a big maple tree that we had lost."

With a more traditional journal, information would have been gathered on the pages as I went along, but the pockets let me put the information where I would refer back to it easily."

New Learning Notebook

for Fran Loges

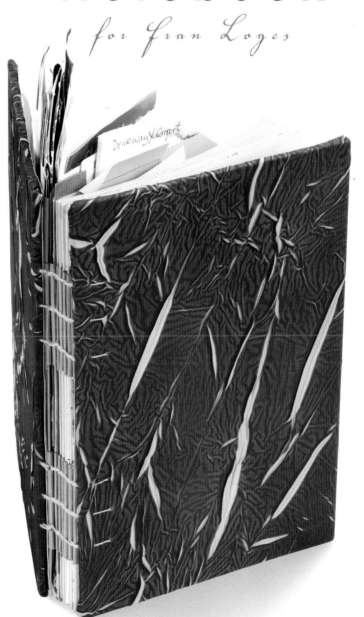

Driveway/Carport

Fran Loges, recently retired after many years of teaching young children, was embarking on a study of landscape architecture. Her learning lab would be her own new construction site, where she and her partner Jim were building a house that Jim had designed. Fran was in charge of the plantings and garden design. She had spent about a year making an informal study of plants and landscape planning, but felt that she needed to be more organized. She thought some kind of notebook or box/notebook combination might help her with this, by making it easier to store and access the many clippings, maps, and drawings she was amassing.

Design Inventory

Fran imagined working on her project at home as well as out on the site, and in garden centers and markets. She said she would typically be writing, doing a little sketching, pasting in flat things, mapping, and collecting seeds and flyers, and pictures and articles. She expected that this box/book could help her make decisions, remember what she had learned, problem solve, and plan. "It will help me break down the landscape learning project into smaller, more manageable parts," she explained.

Choose Your Own Bookbinding Adventure

Here's how things worked out for Fran when she went through the Adventure process:

In section A, she decided she didn't need a fold-over book because that seemed too cumbersome with all the material she envisioned being held within the book. So she went to section C.

In section C, she made the choice for the book to open and stay flat, which took her next to section H.

She didn't think she would need to remove and replace the pages themselves, so she then went to section K.

She knew that one of the chief uses of the book would be to collect and sort information, so she chose to be able to add elements. This choice took her to section T.

In section T, she considered the spine of the book. She thought an open, uncovered spine would make the book more flexible and perhaps better suited to holding lots of added elements, so she went to section V.

Section V suggested she make a Coptic binding with either stubs or a concertina. She decided the concertina might be best, as it would afford some spine protection, which might come in handy when she laid the book down on the muddy ground from time to time. She also opted for a piggyback pamphlet to slip into the main journal so she would have something small and portable to take to the garden center or when she visited different kinds of gardens to get ideas.

A Coptic binding works with either a hard or a flexible cover. Fran chose a hard cover so she could sometimes work while standing up and still have a firm surface on which to write or map or sketch. She thought a Three-Hole Coptic would be sturdier and a good choice for this book, which would have to endure a lot of stress on the binding from its many extra elements.

Fran chose to use a smooth but sturdy paper for writing and collaging (Nidiggan) and also a different one that was strong enough to be sewn or glued together into envelopes in the back part of the book (Canson Mi-Tientes). Browsing in a used bookstore, Fran found a book about Japanese textiles with a beautiful cloth cover that reminded her of cracked soil. The cloth had been top-coated with a varnish so it was less fragile than it looked. It turned out to be water-repellent as well, so she bought the book to use for cover boards.

Insights Gained

After working in her book for a couple of months, Fran brought it to me. It was literally bursting at the seams! It reminded me of a flower bud exploding into bloom. Fran said, "Keeping the journal helped me get organized. That is a change I can use! It took me a while to get used to keeping everything in one place. I am the Post-it type, and would grab little pieces of paper anywhere and write things down, which turns out to be very frustrating when you can't find the information you wrote down. This journal, once I got used to grabbing for it, helped me keep it all in one place. Well, really two places—the main book and the 'mini' that I kept in my purse."

Did the Form Work?

I wondered if and how the form of the book had worked for Fran. She said that the different kinds of paper and spaces in the book gave her ideas that she would not have thought to incorporate into a book. "My project had many facets to it, so organization was a key. Of course, the place for traditional journaling was great, but there were other features that also really worked well for me. I was surprised at how much I used the pockets. I was

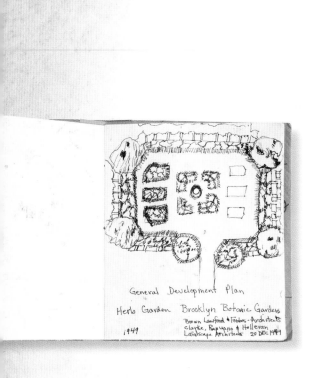

General Development Plan

Herb Garden Brooklyn Botanic Gardens

Brown Lawford & Forbes - Architects
Clarke, Rapuano & Holleran
Landscape Architects   20 DEC 1949

1949

CLEAN PAPER

Clean Paper

FUTURE IDEAS
• Photo
• Garden Gate
  Entry Idea

Portable mini

able to label the different pockets (using the front of the pocket for one topic and the back for another), and as I worked on my pet aspect of a project, I had a place to put the things I gathered (as I started the project) and then a good way to refer back to them as I needed." For example, when Fran was working on the berms, she referred to the "berm" pocket where she had tucked relevant photos, scale drawings, and magazine articles. She didn't have to flip through the journal to track down this information.

The book form complemented the juggling she was doing, working on several aspects of the landscaping project at different times. "With a more traditional journal, information would have been gathered on the pages as I went along, but the pockets let me put the information where I would refer back to it easily."

I asked Fran if there had been any changes in the quality of her attention to the project that she could attribute to keeping this kind of journal. She said, "This journal forced me to get more organized, and I think that helped a great deal with a project of this magnitude. I would have been lost and discouraged long ago if I had not had a good system of recording and keeping track of all the incredible information I was gathering. The journal also let me go back and focus on one small part of the project, adding to or changing something easily. In addition, I found myself turning to the book at night at home, away from the field—looking through it, planning for the next day, the next steps."

Fran said that the journal was wonderful in so many ways. It was practical because she could carry it into the field and not worry if it got dirty. She carried the mini book in her purse, so she could take notes at the nursery or other places where she saw useful information. She also liked the book because it was beautiful. "I loved the cover; it is just so interesting to look at, to feel. I love that feature, even in something so practical. For me, the only thing I would change would be to add more pockets. I have them stuffed."

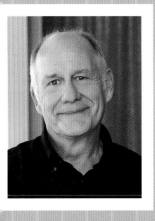

Relationship Journal
for Micah and Rob Pulleyn

When I invited Rob Pulleyn and his daughter Micah to participate in this book, they said it was a perfect time for them to reflect on and explore their relationship: Micah had recently married and was expecting her first baby; Rob was just getting used to being the parent of an adult and suddenly was about to become a grandparent. They thought keeping a journal together would give them a place and a focus for exploring where they were in their own relationship during a period of dramatic life changes. As Micah said: "it would be a place for healing, learning, questioning, connecting, and reflecting… on my relationship with my father and on the future adventure of becoming a parent."

Design Inventory

Micah, an experienced maker of handmade books, wanted the book form to symbolize two voices, two perspectives. She thought that having two spines would help convey that: "I see a book that has one broad back cover with the two front covers that meet in the middle, spines on either side. No traditional foredge—the pages meet in the middle." Rob and Micah imagined working on the book in their homes as well as outside, in the woods, or overlooking Rob's gardens, if they were at his house. They thought they would work on it separately sometimes and occasionally together. The binding would allow two pages to be seen at one time.

As for the kinds of activities they would do in the book, they saw themselves reflecting through writing and artwork. Rob, a ceramicist and artistic doodler, wanted the book to encourage drawing, collage, and photography.

They thought the cover should be able to acquire a patina from use. Rob hoped the cover would lend itself to layering: "The act of remembering is a process of peeling back layers," he explained, "and I'd like a cover that would mirror that idea." They wanted papers that would invite particular kinds of reflection. "Dad loves drafting paper and loves to sketch ideas for his work, his architectural dreams, designs, typography, etc. He and I both love maps—and have traveled in Europe together throughout my life… We are fond of oil pastels, so it would be good to have some thicker, more substantial paper (also good for collage and pictures). Both of us are rather wordy with writing, so a simple paper to write on—but not too large—could be the bulk of the paper."

They further stipulated that they loved deep reds, purples, and mustardy yellows, and that the use of wood, clay, and/or other natural materials would be a plus. Micah also wanted some pages that had been prepared with poured fluid acrylics in these colors.

Choose Your Own Bookbinding Adventure

The Adventure process elicited the following information:

In section A, they decided they did NOT need a fold-around cover, so we proceeded to section C.

In section C, they agreed that they needed the book to open and stay flat, which directed us to section H.

In section H, they chose NOT to remove or replace potentially all of the pages in the book, so we went next to section K.

In section K, they chose to be able to easily add elements, such as drafting or grid paper. We then went to section T.

In section T, they decided they did not need a closed spine but preferred an open spine with decorative, colorful stitching, so we went next to section V.

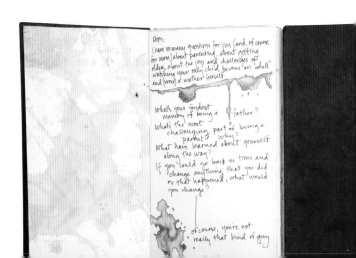

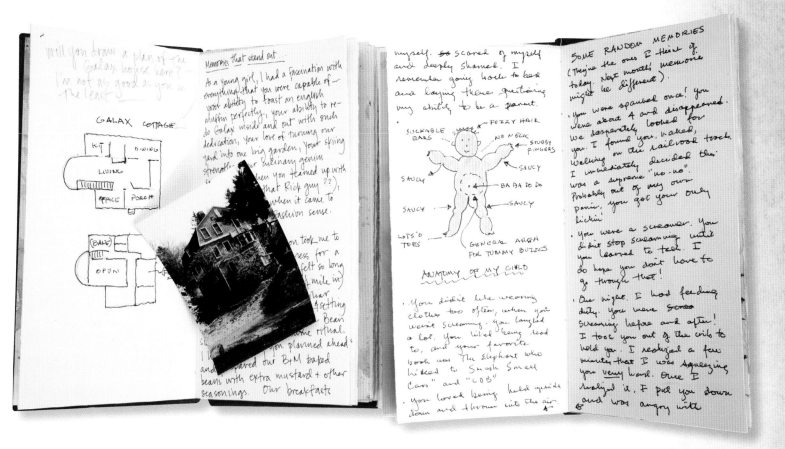

Insights Gained

Section V revealed that the best binding style for them would be a Coptic binding with either a concertina or with stubs added, and that this book could be done as a double book, exactly what they had thought of in the beginning. When they turned to directions for a Coptic binding, they decided to use the concertina since it would not only provide stubs for adding elements, but would help protect the pages that would be exposed by the open spine. The directions for a hard Coptic cover gave modifications to make a double book.

After Micah and Rob had kept their journal for a couple of months, they reflected on the process. Micah said that the project had "helped me realize the intensity of feeling and the depth of questioning I have in becoming a parent, especially as I look in the rearview mirror upon my own life." She said that the project "seemed to show me that there's a lot to explore. I feel like it's just the beginning."

Rob took the opportunity to not only tell stories of his early parenting adventure with Micah, but also to dispense advice to help her develop her own style of parenting with her new baby. He drew wonderful cartoon-like pictures

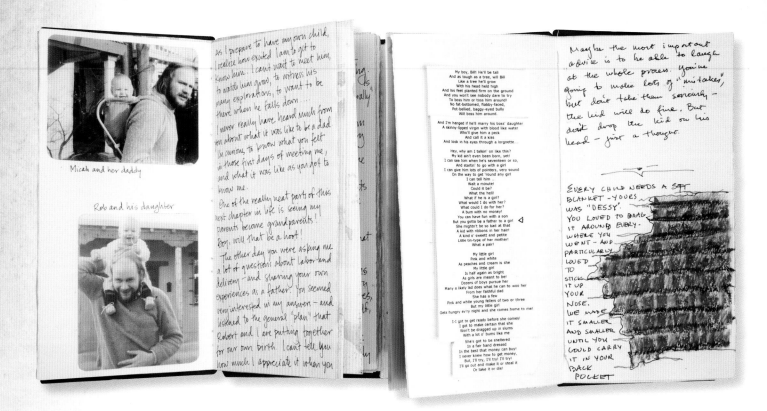

Did the Form Work?

of Micah's special blanket, as well as an "Anatomy of my child," which included the locations for all the lovely funny rituals parents develop with their babies—suckable ears and saucy knees and the general area for the all-important tummy buzzes. His stories included diagrams of the settings of Micah's childhood, and drawings, such as Micah as The Walking Sleeping Bag.

Rob added in a double-page tracing paper map of travels with Micah, which he annotated on the underneath page. Meanwhile, Micah wrote about her interpretation and point of view of many of the same events. She wrote to Rob, asking him to draw floor plans of one of their houses, and then went on to tell stories that happened in the rooms of that house.

Micah said the project had encouraged her to return to the process of journaling, even though she felt rusty. She and Rob agreed that the structure of the book helped remind them of the many conversations they've shared and continue to share.

Rob summed up their experience: "We really enjoyed the exchange of ideas and perspectives the book form invited. When I was putting things into the journal, so many specific events and stories came back to me, some of which Micah and I remembered *very* differently, and that was fun, too." Father and daughter are eager to continue working in the journal together. Rob imagines that when Micah's son, Cole, is older, "he'll be inspired by the journal and the relationship between father and child it reflects, and will one day make a similar journal with his mother."

Group Journal

for Mary Daugherty

This has been our special project—the five little boys and Grandma. It has encouraged us to think and talk about each other, and make things for each other. "

Five of Mary Daugherty's grandsons are between the ages of two and six. Two of them live in Chicago and the other three live a few hours away, near Mary in Michigan. One of Mary's greatest wishes is to build strong relationships among the little cousins as well as, of course, between herself and the children. She thought that a group book might help do that.

Since Mary spends a lot of time with the children and is very inventive at planning outings and activities, she thought it might be good to keep a log of the activities of the Michigan group, which she could then carry back and forth to share with the other cousins when she traveled to see them. She would also keep records of the Chicago boys' outings and visits to show to their Michigan cousins. On the occasions when all the cousins were together, they could work together in the book.

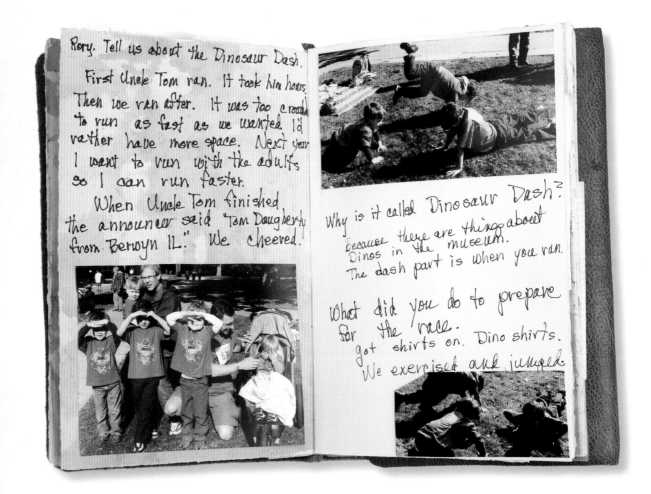

Rory. Tell us about the Dinosaur Dash.

First Uncle Tom ran. It took him hours. Then we ran after. It was too crowded to run as fast as we wanted. I'd rather have more space. Next year I want to run with the adults so I can run faster.

When Uncle Tom finished, the announcer said "Tom Daugherty from Berwyn IL." We cheered!

Why is it called Dinosaur Dash? Because there are things about Dinos in the museum. The dash part is when you ran.

What did you do to prepare for the race. got shirts on. Dino shirts. We exercised and jumped.

Design Inventory

Mary envisioned herself working with the journal at home, at her daughter's or son's house, or at an outdoor setting, such as a park. She pictured the grandchildren drawing, painting, collecting, or doing rubbings directly in the book; she knew she'd write in it to record their activities. She imagined that the book might focus on a group project, but that it would also function as an aid to memory, a means of communication between the two sets of children, and a tool to help forge a group identity.

Mary wanted the book to be strong enough to stand up to hard use. The cover needed to be strong and she wanted it to incorporate photos of all five boys. She also wanted it to fold over so that pencils could be tucked inside and found objects could be carried. She thought a 5½ x 8½-inch (14 x 21.6 cm) page would be large enough for small children to work on, yet still small enough to be portable. She wanted many different kinds of paper—colored, grid, and tracing—to stimulate the boys' interest in doing different kinds of things. Mary also wanted a way to add in extra elements, such as printouts of photographs. She also liked the idea of gluing in an envelope for each boy to use as a personal mailbox for sending notes back and forth among the cousins.

Choose Your Own Bookbinding Adventure

Here's how Mary's Adventure turned out:

In section A, she agreed that she did not need a fold-over cover, which led her to section C.

In section C, she chose a book that would open flat and stay flat, which led her to section H.

In section H, she said, no, she did not need to remove or replace pages in the journal, so she then went to section K.

In section K, she chose to add some pages of special paper to the book, which directed her to section T.

Mary thought a closed spine would be right for this book, so she next went to section U.

In section U, Mary learned about two binding styles that would give her what she wanted: one that was Sewn on Tapes with a concertina, and the other with Accordion Sewn on Tapes. She chose the Sewn on Tapes with a concertina binding because the small folds of the concertina could be used to glue different kinds of paper, envelopes, or flat elements into the book, and there would still be many plain pages. With this binding style, Mary had a few cover choices. She decided a soft leather cover would give protection from the rough treatment the book might receive. It would also make a fold-over possible, a feature that offers even more protection of the pages, as well as a convenient place to store pencils. When she read the directions for a flexible cover, she liked the idea that she could have windows on the cover to hold photos of her grandsons.

Insights Gained

A month later, Mary sent her journal back to me. I hardly recognized it! Mary and the boys smiled out from the cover pictures. Inside, the pages were alive with drawings, maps, photographs, dictated stories, and even pasted-in paper napkins with drawings on them.

I asked Mary how this journal had changed her relationship with the boys and theirs with each other. She said, "It gave us a place to come together, to focus, to plan. Keeping the journal encouraged us to explore themes—collecting leaves, drawing them and doing rubbings of them, making maps of our houses, mixing colors, learning more about dinosaurs."

She explained that six-year-old Nick had been resistant to drawing in the journal until he saw the graph paper and thought about making maps of his house for his cousins. "He got excited about maps, which inspired a lot of back and forth between the cousins," she added. In discussing how the design and form of the book enabled or encouraged them to do things they might not otherwise have done, Mary said, "It gave us many choices: pages to paint on, write on, draw on, make maps on, trace, add on to, and pockets to collect things in. We tend to take a lot of photos. The journal encouraged us to do more artwork and combined media."

I particularly enjoy the pages about the Dinosaur Dash, where Mary transcribed the boys' answers to her interview questions about the event. Photos show all the boys and their fathers getting ready to watch and take part in the race. "Why is it called Dinosaur Dash?" Mary asks the boys. "Because there are things about dinos in the museum. The dash part is where you run!" explains Rory.

Did the Form Work?

Mary said that keeping the journal has strengthened the bond between her and her grandsons: "This has been our special project—the five little boys and Grandma. It has encouraged us to think and talk about each other, and make things for each other." She said that after watching her and the boys work in the journal, her husband, Jim, decided he would like to choose his own 10 favorite things and draw them and write about them. "So we have inspired him, too!" said Mary.

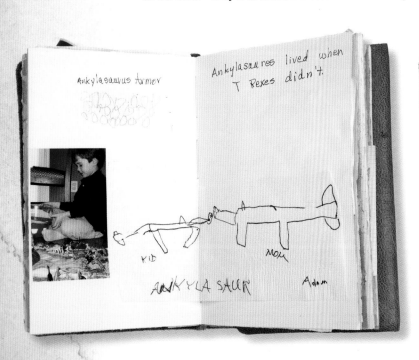

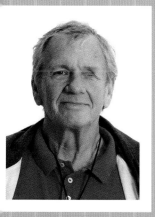

Group Project Notebook

for Chris Kobler

"One of my particular interests is spice, all kinds," Chris Kobler, an experienced and talented amateur chef, told me. He's good at using them, and friends often ask him to share his expertise. "With that in mind," he explained, "I thought a journal devoted to spices would be fun from several perspectives. We could build in sleeves [to hold] vials, envelopes, boxes, papers with seeds and herbs embedded within or glued to the surface, essential oils and so forth."

Chris thought he would start out by using the journal to collect information and recipes and some visuals about spices. Then he imagined using the journal as a centerpiece at dinner parties, a focal point that would let him share his knowledge about spices with his friends, who would, meanwhile, be enjoying foods that were cooked with the spices they were learning about.

Design Inventory

Chris had some novel ideas for the journal. For one thing, he knew from the start that he wanted it to be able to stand up like a desk calendar when he was using it as a centerpiece, and he wanted it to smell spicy and also to have an eccentric and interesting shape. He explained, "It would be interesting if it could be asymmetrical, not outlandish, but maybe like a rakish fez… It does not have to look obviously like a fez; in fact, I'd prefer that it be an abstraction."

Chris thought 40 pages would be adequate, and he wanted a little piggyback journal tucked into the back of the main journal to take along to restaurants. He would need paper in the main book that could withstand collage (printouts of Chris's writing that were glued to the pages). He also planned to glue other things to the pages, among them recipes, sketches, paintings, and spice labels. He didn't think anyone else would be adding things to the journal

before its debut at a dinner party, but he wanted people to be able to add entries later. The main working places for this journal would be in the kitchen and at a worktable.

Choose Your Own Bookbinding Adventure

With all of these requirements in mind, it was time to run Chris's ideas through the Adventure mill.

From the choice in section A, it was clear that Chris needed a flexible binding that would allow him to fold the cover and pages around to the back, for those times when the book had to stand up on the kitchen countertop. The next section was, therefore, section B.

In section B, it seemed clear that the book needed to open and stay flat so that when it was in lying-down mode, it could be more easily worked in or referred to while cooking, so on to section D.

Section D gave the choice of potentially removing and replacing all of the pages. Since Chris wanted to be able to replace some pages with vials and envelopes, we were guided to section F.

Section F suggested a Round-Style Australian Reversed Piano Hinge binding. Since Chris wanted a sturdy, stand-up book, a hard cover with a covered spine seemed the best choice.

Making this book presented some interesting challenges. First of all, in order for the fez-shaped book to be able to stand up, it needed some kind of simple stand to keep the two covers in correct relationship to each other while balancing on one point of each cover. The photo on this page shows the improvised stand that did the job.

Using bamboo barbeque skewers as hinge pins enabled the pages to rotate completely around and flop over to a reasonable degree when the book was in its standing mode. Longer pages would have flopped around more completely under their own weight, but these relatively short pages seemed better at the time, and it didn't seem to be a problem that they partly stood up instead of turning down all the way. Because the text block was attached only to the back cover, it was possible to flip the front cover and spine around to form a sturdy base for the pages.

The book smelled spicy because of the whole peppercorns glued (but not embedded in glue) to the cover. After Chris replaced some pages with little vials of other spices, the smell was even richer.

Insights Gained

After Chris used the journal for a while, I asked him if keeping a journal had changed or enlarged his original project. He said, "It has. I have decided to continue the journal. I have written bits and pieces on food and cooking over time, but they have been project-oriented and without continuity. The journal provides discipline, habit, and becomes its own resource. I have dozens of notebooks around the house with recipes, ideas, and remembrances, and this journal may provide a verbal 'drawer' for all of this."

Did the Form Work?

Chris said the group aspect of his journal ended up taking a back seat and had interfered with his process, because he had to think of how to make things clear to an audience. He now prefers the idea of a solitary journal. However, he said, "The stand-up aspect [of this journal] will work for my friends who want to use the recipes. When the journal is circulated among the group, they will be able to use it in their kitchens or to copy for their own use."

He wants his next journal to have a more conventional design, especially in terms of shape, and be constructed with even heavier paper. He said the fez shape had turned out to be a distraction. He intended to keep his idea of removing some pages and replacing them with vials of spices. However, instead of paper hinges, he'd try cloth ones, which could work if the concertina part of the binding were made of stiff bookcloth, and therefore would be less likely to tear with repeated removing and replacing of the vials. He liked the stand-up aspect, the envelopes, and the open-flat design of the book.

"Overall, keeping this journal has been useful to me. I am curious to see whether the habit of writing food thoughts down will 'take,'" Chris said in conclusion.

I especially like Chris's story because it highlights the advantage of being able to modify a journal and try something slightly different for the next book. It's very difficult to know how something is going to work until you actually use it for a while. When you design and make your own journal, it's possible to fine tune aspects of the design that are less than perfect, while holding onto the aspects that work well. Also, as your project surprises you by growing and changing, you will have the ability to redesign your book to meet the project's new needs.

Emblem Book

for Ann Turkle

Ann Turkle had recently moved across the country. Facing the daunting number of boxes and pieces of furniture that had moved with her, she began to think about a project she had started years ago when her mother was having trouble paring down her possessions. Ann had suggested that her mother draw and write about her treasured furniture and mementos and in this way *emblemize* them. It might, then, be easier to let go of them.

When I invited her to participate in *Real Life Journals*, Ann decided that an emblem book might help her pare down her own possessions. A long-time journal keeper, Ann envisioned the book as "more than the usual receptacle. It stays at home—even on a given shelf—and I bring things to it and get it out to show to people. I imagine myself making sure that things get into it, and thinking, good, now I won't lose that."

Ann saw herself using the book as a system of preservation, a sort of archive or bell jar. "What I think I'll do with the book is not simply collect things, but translate them. So, I have a small silver pin my father got my mother in North Africa that looks like a bit of Arabic script. It could fit into the book/box, but I'd rather do a watercolor of the pin—along with, say, my writing and drawings of leather pillows and hassocks that have long since fallen by the wayside. (It occurs to me that this will allow me to put things together that are too unwieldy to assemble in the flesh—or are gone. What fun!)"

Above all, Ann wanted to diminish her need to hold onto too many things. She didn't want to forget the things, but she did want to make a record of her interactions with them.

Design Inventory

The book itself needed to be a marriage of box and book. Adding and removing pages was important, but as Ann thought about it, she realized that the pages themselves might not actually have to be bound. She wanted pages that could be drawn and written on, and she also wanted envelopes or folders or pockets to hold odds and ends and perhaps a small, foldaway booklet that she could carry to the attic or storage unit. She had some drawings with notes on them that her mother had made years ago, and Ann wanted to model some of her entries on those.

Organization was important to this project, and Ann wanted a page on which she could write a contents list to indicate what was in the book/box. She thought the book should be rather large, about 8½ by 11 inches (21.6 x 27.9 cm) and about 2 inches (5.1 cm) thick, so that it could accommodate large folded pages. She also wanted a cloth-covered hard cover that felt good to hold—she could imagine sitting with her granddaughter on the couch with the book opened out on their laps.

Choose Your Own Bookbinding Adventure

Here's how the Adventure process worked for Ann:

In section A, Ann said that she didn't need a fold over cover, so she went to section C.

In section C, she agreed that the book needed to open and stay flat, which sent her to section H.

In section H, she realized she didn't actually need to remove or replace pages, as long as she could remove and replace items that were tucked inside bound page-envelopes, so she went to section K.

Ann wanted to add at least one two-sided table of contents page to the book, so she turned to section T.

In section T, she decided on a closed, covered spine so that she could write a title of some sort on the spine someday. She also thought a covered spine would look better on its shelf, so she turned to section U.

In section U, Ann learned that there were two styles of binding that would work for her project book: one was a Sewn on Tapes with a concertina, and the other was an Accordion Sewn onto Tapes. Ann thought the idea of turning at least some of the accordion-folded pages into envelopes worked perfectly with her idea of having a place to collect drawings with writing on them—her emblems. She decided on a hard cover and a small piggyback journal to slip into the back of the big book.

Insights Gained

After Ann had used the journal for a couple of months, I asked her how keeping a journal had enlarged or changed her project. She said that while her original aim had been to preserve or curate pieces of her past, she found herself distracted by her present life and ended up enlarging the project to include it.

"I had a writing professor who urged me to get angry at my distractions, but I've never been good at that. I love my distractions. So my garden, which always demands a certain amount of my attention, found its way into the journal, even though I'm not sure it exactly fits the purpose of the book. I kept losing track of what [plants] I bought and when and where they had been planted. So I created a little section in the book devoted to perennials and veggies. Also, the collection of 'family elephants' was not part of my original plan, but they spoke to me and here they are."

Ann's original intention was to assemble the filling for all those pockets, write stories about them, and simply label the items, but then she found herself decorating (in very random ways) the outsides of the pockets. "I imagined sitting down with my granddaughter someday and sharing this journal, and I wanted an easy, visual way of identifying the contents."

Did the Form Work?

I asked her how the design and form of the book had enabled or encouraged her to do things she might not otherwise have done.

Ann said, "As I searched for things to include [in the pockets], I came across items that reminded me I needed to record more stories. If my son, who knows many of the family stories, came across the Eastern Star pins, I'm not sure he'd know what they signify or that they belonged to my mother's mother. I am, quite possibly, the only one aware of the provenance of the elephants. Write it down, write it down, I urged myself, just as I had made the same assignment for my mother."

I asked her what features of the journal worked the best for her and what they facilitated. "The journal is *very* inviting. It's easy to imagine that any single pocket might generate a whole journal of its own, so the contents of the pocket become a journal-in-waiting or beg for a more significant project. The bookmarks alone deserve an illustrated essay. I've never kept a garden journal, but now I may. The other night I found myself half-dreaming of the journal itself as a seed packet, and its contents may germinate and sprout into larger, more significant creations."

Ann explained that she doesn't want to be too much in love with things, but she does want to respect them: "Their stories are the story of my life, the story of my family. The lamp my mother pictured as one of her household items got left behind in North Carolina. It

was never stable and, even if rewired, offered no way to conceal the electric cord. Because I write about it (and my mother drew it) I feel a little less guilty for not dragging it along. A journal that dispels both anxiety and guilt is worth its weight in gold."

I asked Ann if there were any surprises as she kept the journal.

"I was surprised that it became a wonderful way of thinking about my mother. She was a dramatic and flamboyant character, and I had never before thought of her exclusively in terms of what she created. But I was led in that direction by paying attention to her 'household items' sketches, and then to some of the other things she was devoted to, like her dolls and her calligraphy. It's a good way of being reminded of who she was in her essence."

Finally, I asked her if there were any changes in the quality of her attention to the project or things she

noticed that she could attribute to keeping the journal.

Ann explained, "I think the pockets create the potential for focused attention. In a normal journal, I'm able to write about anything whenever I please. But the pockets invite like items to gravitate to them. For instance, I found the clipping about my mother's doll workshop, and I had a place to put it! In fact, each pocket is crying out, 'Feed me! Feed me!' When I create a shadow box for all the pocket watches (and pen knives) I'm heir to, I'll devote a pocket to telling their stories, too."

Ann concluded by saying that if she were to create another journal for this project she might make a couple of changes. She found she didn't use the piggyback journal as she thought she would, because the rest of the journal was flexible enough to carry around. Instead, she might make some very small mini-journals to include in some of the pockets. And because she put more items into the individual pockets than she envisioned, she would give them a more secure closing on their bottom ends.

the basics

Now that you've found the perfect design— possibly something with an inscrutable name like Flat-Style Australian Reversed Piano Hinge—it's time to learn about the bookbinding materials and tools you may need to make your real life journal. This chapter also includes a description of artist materials and techniques you can use to build your journal pages. There are also ideas about how to energize your writing.

The Bookbinding Essentials foldout stored in the envelope inside the back cover features the techniques you'll need to make any book form or cover. These are simple procedures, easy to master. Keep the foldout on your worktable to refer to as you make your journal.

Bookbinding Tools

To make the text blocks and the covers featured in this book, you need the following tools and materials. Most are available in art or craft supply stores, sewing shops, office supply stores, and hardware stores. For a few of the supplies, you may need to contact a bookbinding supply house. Here are two of my favorites: www.talas-nyc.com and www.hollanders.com.

awls

An *awl* is basically a hole-puncher. I recommend a thin one for bookbinding because you often need to punch relatively small holes. In a pinch, you can substitute a pushpin. The thicker awls found in hardware stores can work as long as you don't push them in too far. Store your awl with its tip in an old cork.

bone folders

A *bone folder*, a flat knife-like tool made of bone or Teflon™, is excellent for burnishing surfaces, scoring lines on paper, smoothing the edges of boards, and working adhesive into paper and board. Suitable substitutes include a paper clip for scoring paper and a plastic knife for smoothing edges. Teflon bone folders often have very thick edges, but you can sand them down to taper them.

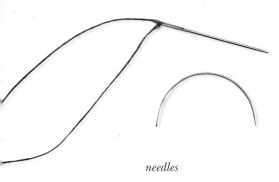

needles

mat knife

glue brushes

In bookbinding, you need two kinds of *needles*, depending on the type of binding you're sewing: a straight needle and a curved needle. Both need relatively large eyes because bookbinder's thread is heavier than most sewing threads. Take your thread to the store with you to make sure the needle's eye is big enough. The needle's body still needs to be as thin as possible to avoid leaving large holes in the paper.

Another important tool is a *straightedge*, used for scoring and tearing paper, for folding concertinas, for taking measurements, and in cutting paper and boards. You can get by with an 18-inch (45.7 cm) metal ruler, but you'll eventually

yearn for the ultimate: a 36-inch (91.4 cm) steel straightedge with a beveled edge for tearing and a square edge for cutting. If you decide to splurge on an expensive one, look in a bookbinding or art supply store.

To make a journal, you also need a *mat knife*—preferably with a snap-off blade—for cutting paper and boards. Heavy-duty knives cut both paper and boards. Smaller knives are not as good for cutting book boards.

Cutting mats come in various sizes, and big ones can be expensive. A new design, made of 6 x 12-inch (15.2 x 30.5 cm) sections, allows you to join pieces like a jigsaw puzzle into long strips, squares, or even L-shapes. One reasonably priced package contains three sections. I bought two packages, and the six sections serve me for every purpose. Beware of very thin cutting mats that don't self-heal and work only with a specific knife. Store your cutting mat in a cool, dark place as it warps when exposed to heat and sunlight. You can also use a large piece of cardboard as a cutting surface.

A *glue brush* is an essential tool. You can use a blunt-tipped stencil brush or an inexpensive 1-inch (2.5 cm) flat brush. Eventually, you may want a beautiful, wooden-handled Japanese glue brush, but you can easily make do with less expensive models.

Certain book form instructions call for binder clips and a C-clamp or two. *Clamps and weights* are certainly handy to have around, but you can easily improvise both. To create a weight, use a pile of books, wrap a brick in cloth, or fill an empty mint tin with pennies. A roll of *waxed paper* is also useful when pressing; put it between the weight and the book, as well as between pages that are still damp with adhesive.

Ordinary *graphite pencils and erasers* are important tools for marking and removing marks from paper, boards, and cover materials. Never mark in ballpoint pen or colored pencil, although for some dark-colored materials such as leather, you may need a white pencil.

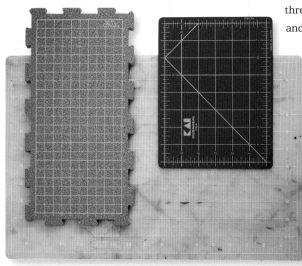

cutting mats

Bookbinding Materials

You can make *book boards* (covers) out of mat board or, even better, out of an inexpensive archival cardboard called *Davey board*. Used by most bookbinders, Davey board comes in three thicknesses. You can buy it at art supply and bookbinding supply stores.

Bookbinder's thread comes in several thicknesses, waxed or unwaxed, and in an array of colors. For hidden thread, such as in a Sewn on Tapes book, use 2-ply white or off-white unwaxed linen. For styles in which thread becomes a decorative element, such as a Coptic book, try a 3-ply thread in a color that complements your design. Some bookbinders prefer waxed linen thread because it tends not to tangle as much and slides smoothly through paper. Since heavily waxed thread can leave an oily mark on the paper next to the stitches, I generally choose unwaxed or lightly waxed thread. You can lightly wax thread yourself with a thread waxer (available at sewing stores) or with a chunk of beeswax.

Binder's tape is a non-adhesive cloth tape that you sew over when joining signatures. You can substitute ½- or ¾-inch-wide (1.3 or 1.9 cm) ribbon. Use a strong type of ribbon, such as cotton or non-shiny grosgrain.

The directions for making an album call for *screw posts*. You can find them at some art or craft supply stores or at an on-line bookbinding supply house.

Paper

Paper is such an important element of bookbinding that it needs more than a brief mention. It interacts with every medium you place on it, from adhesives to inks to paints. It's very useful to understand what paper is and how it works before you buy any. Knowing a few basic facts can help you match the right paper to the materials you want to put on the page.

All paper is made of cellulose-containing fiber. The fiber first undergoes a macerating process that bruises the cellulose fibers so they attract water. The result is pulp. Sometimes chemicals are added to increase the opacity or improve the finish of the resulting paper. *Sizing*, a mild adhesive that inhibits the water-attracting quality of the cellulose, is usually added. Sizing stops liquid media (such as ink or paint) from bleeding. After it's formed into a sheet, the paper is pressed to remove the water, causing the cellulose fibers to form strong chemical bonds across hydrogen molecules. The paper is then dried and sometimes pressed further to smooth the surface.

The fibers in machine-made sheets line up more or less parallel to each other because the papermaking machinery shakes it in one direction. The direction of the fibers is called the *grain* of the paper. Handmade paper doesn't have grain because it's not shaken this way.

Davey board

bookbinder's thread

binder's tape

screw posts

JUDITH GOLDEN *Albuquerque Journal,* **2007**
11¾ x 8¾ x ¾ inches (30 x 22.2 x 1.9 cm); book sewn over decorative tapes PHOTO BY PAT BARRETT

PAPER	Arches Cover	Arches Text	Strathmore 500 Series Drawing Paper	Strathmore 400 Series Drawing Paper	Vellum	Grid paper
USE WITH						
PEN	yes	yes	yes	yes	yes	yes
WATERCOLOR	yes	yes	light	light	no	no
PENCIL	yes	yes	yes	yes	yes	yes
COLLAGE	yes	yes	light	light	no	no
TRACING	no	no	no	no	yes	no
ACRYLIC	yes	yes	light	light	no	light
WHERE TO FIND	art, craft, online	art, craft, online	art, craft, online	art, craft, online	art, craft, online	art, craft, drafting, office

When fibers in grained papers become wet, they swell slightly in a direction perpendicular to the grain. Then, as the paper dries, the fibers lose water and the sheet shrinks. When this paper is wet unevenly—such as when you paint on or apply adhesive to a part of it—it curls, buckles, and wrinkles from uneven swelling and shrinking. In general, the heavier the paper, the flatter it dries.

Paper is somewhat fragile. It's affected by what happens on its surface as well as by the humidity of the air around it. So respect each sheet's limitations. Match the paper to the media you'll use on it. Wet media, including wet adhesives, are particularly hard on paper. Anything containing water reverses the papermaking process to a degree: the fibers absorb water and swell. The bonds between individual fibers weaken. Drying then shrinks the fibers to a slightly different size than they were before, which can warp the paper.

Watercolor paper is made to withstand being wet and re-wet without undue stretching and buckling, as long as you dry it under restraint. Heavier-bodied watercolor paper has sufficient sizing to control absorbency and help the matting of its surface fibers stand up to scrubbing and even scratching.

Drawing paper comes in different weights and finishes, all specifically made for pen, pencil, and even light watercolor work, such as watercolor sketching. Regardless, don't ask it to absorb as much water as watercolor paper or to stand up to repeated washings.

Vellum is beautiful translucent paper with a smooth, low-porous surface, but it requires special considerations. Made by overbeating cellulose fibers to form a jelly, vellum has very short fibers, so it reacts more severely to moisture and temperature than conventional papers. It buckles and curls when wet, so use drier adhesives, such as glue sticks. You can write on it with all kinds of inks, but inks take a little longer to dry because of the low porosity of the paper. Watercolor, gouache (opaque watercolors), acrylics, and inks all adhere to vellum, but they cause some buckling and cockling if spread over a large area. You can print on vellum in an inkjet printer, but not in a laser printer because the heat causes the paper to curl and frizz.

Paper used as the base of a *collage* needs to be heavy enough to support the weight of the elements attached to it plus the adhesives used. Lightweight papers curl and wrinkle when you apply wet adhesives. You'll

Magnani Velata, 120 lb.	Lokta (handmade)	Niddigan (tan)	Heavy Resume Paper	Computer Paper	Canson MiTientes	PAPER
						USE WITH
yes	yes	yes	yes	yes	yes	**PEN**
yes	light	light	light	no	light	**WATERCOLOR**
yes	yes	yes	yes	yes	yes	**PENCIL**
yes	light	light	light	no	light	**COLLAGE**
no	no	no	no	no	no	**TRACING**
yes	yes	yes	light	light	yes	**ACRYLIC**
art, online	art, online	art, online	office supply	office supply	art, craft, online	**WHERE TO FIND**

achieve the best results by using a relatively heavy paper as the base of a collage while attaching lighter elements to it.

There are literally thousands of kinds of paper. The above table includes papers you can easily find. Whenever you discover a new type of paper that interests you, buy only a small amount at first to try out with the various mediums you plan to use.

Adhesives

The adhesives discussed here will satisfy most of your needs in bookbinding and journal keeping.

PVA (polyvinyl acetate) is a thick, white liquid adhesive that comes in a plastic bottle. The best way to use it is to pour some into a small bowl and apply with a glue brush. Marketed under a number of brand names, PVA comes in school quality, craft grade, or high quality. School quality PVA is not suitable for bookbinding, but craft quality works just fine. High-quality PVAs—about twice as expensive as the craft grade—are strong, the easiest to spread, dry the most flexible, and are the least likely to wrinkle paper. PVA is low-odor, acid-free, dries relatively quickly, and cleans up with water while it's wet.

All PVAs are relatively wet adhesives; items adhere quickly with PVA and are difficult or impossible to reposition. Use them with care; they stain bookcloth and paper, leaving a shiny, impossible-to-remove mark when dry.

Glue sticks are handy for collage and for attaching found materials in a journal. They are inexpensive and relatively dry. There are acid-free kinds that come in both permanent and repositionable formulas. For most bookbinding jobs, use the permanent variety. Glue sticks don't create a bond as strong as PVA, but they're fine for adhering two surfaces that won't be subjected to stress (so don't use them to attach a strap to a cover, for instance). Also, they dry too quickly to use for covering book

BRUCE KREMER *28–29Jan95*, 1995
8 x 11 inches (20.3 x 27.9 cm); combined materials in a diary PHOTO BY ARTIST

boards. Depending on the brand, they can be long lasting, acid free, fast drying, and guaranteed to not wrinkle paper, even vellum. Most adhere porous paper to non-porous surfaces, such as mica and plastic.

Similar to a glue stick, *YES paste* is a thick white paste that's easier to spread over a large surface because it dries more slowly. It is permanent but reversible, and it doesn't stain. YES cleans up with water. It creates a stronger bond than a glue stick, but it's still a weaker adhesive than PVA.

Drymount tissue can also be used as a dry adhesive that won't wrinkle paper (except for vellum, which can't take the heat involved in dry mounting). Trim a piece about $\frac{1}{16}$ inch (1.6 mm) smaller than the perimeter of the materials you want to adhere, and then sandwich it in between. Lay a piece of scrap paper over the top sheet and gently press with a warm iron set at permanent press for a few minutes. If you join paper and cloth, the result is heavy, cover-weight bookcloth that is ideal for covering book boards (page 49). You can buy drymount tissue from photographic supply houses, as its primary use is to mount photographs to boards.

Bookcloth

You can buy bookcloth lined with paper or treated with glue or heavy sizing. Treat unlined book cloth as a grain-free material and paper-lined bookcloth as a grained material. To avoid warped book boards, see the Bookbinding Essentials. You can find

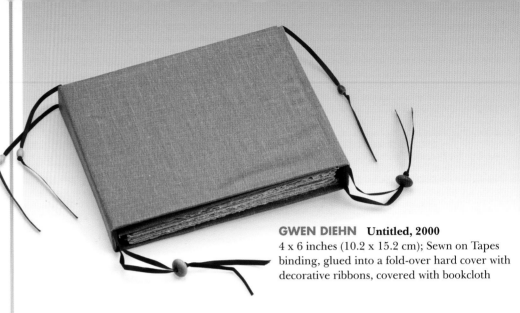

bookcloth at some art supply stores, but the best sources are online from the major bookbinding supply houses.

You can, however, make your own bookcloth from ordinary cloth, but you must first line it to prevent adhesives from bleeding through the weave and staining the front of the board. To line the cloth, cut it to size and then cut a sheet of light paper to the same size. Cut a piece of drymount tissue about $\frac{1}{16}$ inch (1.6 mm) smaller in all dimensions. Sandwich the drymount tissue between the cloth and paper. After placing a piece of clean scrap paper over the cloth, iron for a few minutes with a regular iron set at permanent press. The iron melts the drymount tissue, sealing the paper to the cloth. If you used grained paper as a lining, treat the homemade bookcloth as you would grained paper. Only handmade paper is ungrained (see Bookbinding Essentials).

GWEN DIEHN **Untitled, 2000**
4 x 6 inches (10.2 x 15.2 cm); Sewn on Tapes binding, glued into a fold-over hard cover with decorative ribbons, covered with bookcloth

Headbands

Headbands were originally the rows of stitching at the top and bottom of a book's spine between the cover and text block—the last stitches on either end of the book. Linked together to form a decorative braid, they also played a structural function: protecting binding inside the spine from dust while strengthening the stitching. Very few bookbinders sew real headbands anymore, although it's possible to buy headband material from major bookbinding suppliers. It's also easy to make your own decorative headbands.

If you want a book with a Sewn on Tapes binding, with either a hard or flexible cover, with or without a concertina, a headband makes a nice finishing touch. Here's how to make your own.

headband

Making Your Own Headbands

WHAT YOU NEED

Bookbinding Tool Kit (page 47)

Text block for a Sewn on Tapes book, backed and ready to be glued to the cover

Patterned or colored cloth or paper, 2 x 5 inches (5.1 x 12.7 cm)

String, about 5 inches (12.7 cm) long

Scrap paper

Rag

WHAT YOU DO

1. Brush PVA completely over the inside of the 2 x 5-inch (5.1 x 12.7 cm) piece of cloth or paper.

2. Lay the string down the long center of the cloth or paper. Fold the cloth or paper in half, so the string forms a ridge in the fold (figure 1).

3. Use the bone folder to burnish the cloth or paper tight against the string. You want the ridge of the string to be apparent.

4. When the PVA is dry, cut the cloth or paper into two sections, each the exact width of the spine of the text block (figure 2).

5. Brush a little PVA on one side of the headband (figure 3).

6. Press the headband against the spine of the text block so the ridge protrudes $\frac{1}{16}$ inch (1.6 mm) or so above the text block (figure 4).

7. Turn to the cover instructions (page 147) and glue the text block into the book cover.

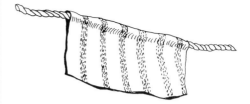

figure 1

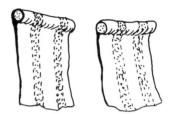

figure 2

figure 3

figure 4

GWEN DIEHN **Journal, 2001**
$3\frac{1}{2}$ x 5 x $1\frac{1}{4}$ inches (8.9 x 12.7 x 3.2 cm); Sewn on Tapes glued into a leather cover with fold-over and tie; pen

figure 5

figure 6

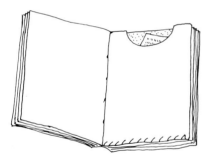

figure 7

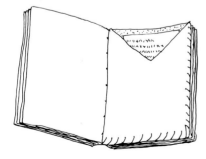

figure 8

KERSTIN VOGDES *Costa Rica/Nicaragua Journal, 2008*
6 x 6 inches (15.2 x 15.2 cm); soft corrugated paper cover with Multiple Pamphlets and concertina, envelope converted from a deep concertina fold

Making Envelopes

Envelopes are useful in many journals. This section presents several ways of binding them in or adding them to a book.

Binding in an envelope. If your book has folios, simply fold a top-opening envelope in half and sew it in the center fold of the signature. You must either remove the envelope flap first or else cut it at the fold so it's easy to open once it's bound in (figure 5).

Tipping in an envelope. You'll need a binding with a concertina fold or a stub for this method. If your book doesn't have a stub or fold, you can make one by cutting the next page into a 1-inch (2.5 cm) stub. Then use YES paste (page 52) or PVA (page 51) to attach the side or bottom of the envelope to the stub (figure 6).

Converting an accordion fold. If your book has a page-sized accordion fold where you want an envelope, simply sew or glue the bottom of the fold. You also may want to trim the front of the envelope opening to make it easier to use (figure 7). To reinforce the closure at the bottom, sew it closed with two rows of stitching or use a stick-on label to reinforce the bottom seam.

Using two pages as an envelope. Sew or glue the bottoms and the foredges together (figure 8). Reinforce the seams as needed.

Adding Windows to a Flexible Cover

Some journal keepers like to add one or more windows for drawings or photographs (see example on page 35).

WHAT YOU NEED

Bookbinding Tool Kit (page 47)

Cover material, cut to size

Acetate, ½ inch (1.3 cm) longer and wider than the planned window (for Method #1) or 1 inch (2.5 cm) wider than the window (for Method #2)

PVA or YES paste (page 51)

Lining paper, ½ inch (1.3 cm) longer and wider than the acetate

Photograph, drawing, title card, pressed plant, etc., to put in the window

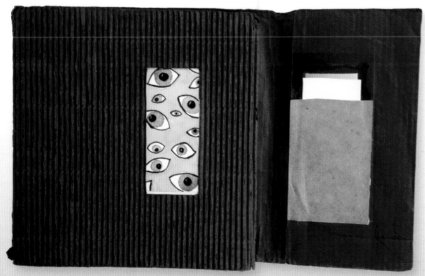

KERSTIN VOGDES *Costa Rica/Nicaragua Journal,* 2008
6 x 6 inches (15.2 x 15.2 cm); soft corrugated paper cover with Multiple Pamphlets and concertina sewn directly to the cover; watercolor, pen, ink—a good example of windows in a flexible cover

WHAT YOU DO (METHOD #1)

1. You must make the windows in the cover *before* you sew, lace, or glue in the text block. Decide where to put the window(s) on the cover. For each window, draw the outline on the inside of the cover material.

2. Cut out the window opening completely. Lay the piece of acetate over the opening and affix it to the cover material in the ½-inch (1.3 cm) overlapping area on all four sides with the paste or PVA (figure 9).

3. If you want a permanent picture or title card in the window(s), skip ahead to step 4. If you want to be able to change the picture, continue with this step. Lay the piece of lining paper over the acetate, leaving the top ⅛ inch (3 mm) uncovered (figure 10). Paste the overlapping lining paper on the sides and bottom but not at the top. Trim a picture or title card, leaving a little extra at the top edge. Slide it into the pocket (figure 11), and you can change it whenever you want.

4. If you want a permanent picture, drawing, or title card to show in the window, lay the picture face down on top of the acetate, and then lay the lining paper over the picture. Glue the four overlap edges of the lining paper to form a sealed pocket for the picture (figure 12).

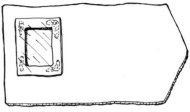

figure 9

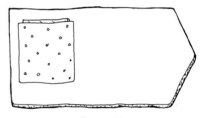

figure 10

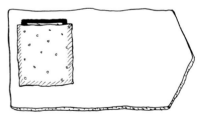

figure 11

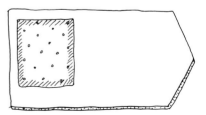

figure 12

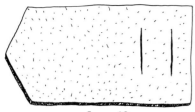

figure 13

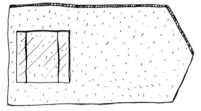

figure 14

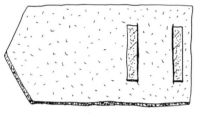

figure 15

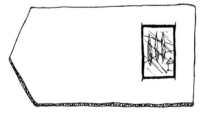

figure 16

WHAT YOU DO (METHOD #2)

1. You must make the windows in the cover *before* you sew, lace, or glue in the text block. Decide where to put the window(s) on the cover. For each window, make two cuts right through the cover material, one on either side of the window opening (figure 13). You are not cutting out a window opening, just making slits into which you can slide the acetate.

2. Double-check that the acetate is 1 inch (2.5 cm) wider than the space between the two slits and exactly as high as the height of the two slits (figure 14). Either trim the acetate or adjust the size of the slits if necessary.

3. Slide the acetate into place from the inside to the outside and back again. On the inside, paste the overlapping area of the acetate, pressing it firmly to the cover material (figure 15). The end sheets of the text block, when glued in place, will cover the raw edges of the acetate.

4. To insert a photograph or title card, first trim it to the width and height of the acetate (as measured from outside the cover). Slip the picture behind the acetate from the front of the book (figure 16).

Adding Windows to a Hard Cover

In a hardcover book, the window(s) you make become a permanent part of the cover. I recommend minimizing the number of windows, as too many weaken the cover. See Rebecca Casey's journal (page 57) for an example of this kind of window.

MARY DAUGHERTY *Grandchildren Journal,* **2009**
5½ x 8½ inches (14 x 21.6 cm); detail of window in a flexible cover

WHAT YOU NEED

Bookbinding Tool Kit (page 47)

Cover boards, cut to size but uncovered

Cloth or paper covering material

PVA or YES paste (page 51)

Acetate, mica, rawhide, or other transparent or translucent material you like, ½ inch (1.3 cm) longer and wider than the window

Photograph, drawing, title card, pressed plant, etc., to put in the window

WHAT YOU DO

1. Decide where to put the window(s) on the cover. For each window, draw the outline on the cover board. Cut out the window opening with a craft knife.

2. Cover the boards as instructed in the Bookbinding Essentials (figure 17). Note that you will cover over the window at this point.

3. After the covered boards have dried, draw an "X" in the window opening from the inside of the cover (figure 18).

4. From the inside of the cover, cut through the lines you drew in step 3. Carefully brush paste onto the triangles formed when you cut the "X." Fold each triangle back over the edge of the window (figure 19). Burnish thoroughly.

5. Lay the piece of acetate over the window opening on the inside of the board. Paste the overlapping areas and burnish the acetate to the board (figure 20).

6. Trim the photograph, drawing, title card, pressed plant, or other object of your choice

so it fits perfectly in the window. Place it face down on top of the acetate.

7. Continue by gluing the text block in place. The end pages, when glued in place, will seal the picture into the window.

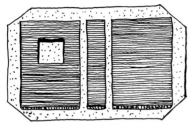

figure 17

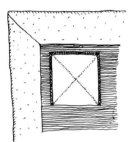

figure 18

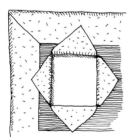

figure 19

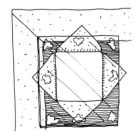

figure 20

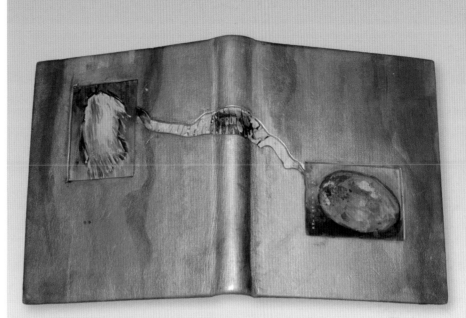

WENDY HALE DAVIS *Fruition*, **2009**
8¾ x 15¾ x 1¼ inches (22.2 x 40 x 3.2 cm); full leather dyed with metallic ink over boards, gouache insets PHOTO BY WENDY OGLE

REBECCA CASEY
Watercolor/Meditation Journal, **2008**
7 x 7 x 2½ inches (17.8 x 17.8 x 6.4 cm); hardcover book with a window

Encrusting a Hard Cover

Another option for changing a hard cover is to encrust it with sand, soil, seeds, crayon shavings, or even eggshells. Use a hard cover because a flexible cover will crack the encrustation.

WHAT YOU NEED

Bookbinding Tool Kit (page 47)

Encrusting material (e.g., soil, rice, powdered pigments, crayon shavings, crushed eggshells, or sand)

Mortar and pestle or rolling pin and a tough plastic bag

Acrylic matte medium

Water

Whiting powder or calcium carbonate (optional)

Masking tape

Hardcover journal

Scrap paper

Palette or putty knife (or pieces of stiff mat board or cardboard cut to 1 x 2 inches [2.5 to 5.1 cm])

Rags

Acrylic paints (optional, see Note)

Paste wax (optional, see Note)

Sandpaper (optional, see Note)

Note: Some of the tools and materials above are optional, since encrustations can take so many forms.

WHAT YOU DO

1. Before mixing components together, first grind any soil, eggshells (with the membranes removed), or other lumpy material that you want to use. Use a mortar and pestle—or a rolling pin and a tough plastic bag.

2. Mix the acrylic medium with the encrusting material to form a plaster with putty-like consistency. Whiting, available at art and craft supply stores, helps to thicken the encrustation, but you can do without it.

3. Put a piece of masking tape along the book's spine. Lay a sheet of scrap paper between the cover and the first page of the text block to protect it (figure 21).

4. Apply the putty-like mixture to the book's cover in thin coats, letting it dry between coats. If you *want* the surface to crack, however, apply a thick coat.

5. Allow the encrustation to dry completely. This can take up to 24 hours, depending on its thickness, the humidity, and the room temperature.

6. If you want, you can add more coats, sand the encrustation, wax it, paint it with acrylics, or even carve into it. You can probably think of many other things to do as well, and all of them are effective.

7. When you're satisfied with the encrustation, use acrylics to paint the raw board edges as well as inside the cover (figure 22).

figure 21

figure 22

Making Ties

Some journal keepers like to add ties to keep their journals firmly closed. A very simple way to make a tie is to cut the front flap of the cover so that it has a long tail attached. Below is another simple way to make a tie.

WHAT YOU NEED

Bookbinding Tool Kit (page 47)

Piece of leather about ½ inch (1.3 cm) wide and 3½ times as long as the width of the book

WHAT YOU DO

1. Carefully cut two slits into the flap of the cover (figure 23).

2. Tie a knot on one end of the leather tie.

3. Thread the unknotted end of the tie through the slits (figure 24) to hold it in place. Wrap the tie around the book.

4. Tuck the tapered end of the tie under the wrapped part (figure 25).

figure 23

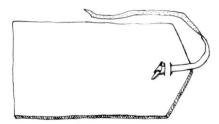

figure 24

figure 25

GWEN DIEHN   *Scary Bomarzo Journal,* 2007
6 x 5 x 1 inches (15.2 x 12.7 x 2.5 cm); bookcloth-covered spine, cover encrusted with sand, local clay, acrylic medium

LEILA SCOGIN
Little Memories Book, 2008
4 x 2½ x ½ inches (10.2 x 6.4 x 1.3 cm); handmade leather-bound book with rope tie; mixed media

LAURIE CORRAL   *Travel Journal,* 2005
5 x 8 inches (12.7 x 20.3 cm); leather straps, button, multimedia paper; collage, absorbant ground, pen

Page-Building Materials

Journal pages, clearly, can take myriad and unexpected forms. Be aware that you'll often work pages in a book on both sides. Also remember that turning pages and pressing on already-worked pages stress whatever medium you've used on the paper.

The materials listed here dry completely and won't rub off or smear onto facing pages. They also won't bleed through most papers. Finally, most of these supplies are acid-free or archival quality, so they won't degrade paper over time.

Pen and ink is a basic medium for writing or drawing in your journal. Fine-tipped steel, gel, or metallic pens come in many types. There are many inks to choose from, too. Find out for yourself which ones feel and look best to you.

Pencils and erasers are essential tools. You'll write and draw with them. Avoid extremely soft pencils because they smear easily; a good range is between 3B and 2H. Keep a pencil sharpener handy, and don't scrimp on a good eraser.

Colored pencils are an easy way to bring color into your journal. You can mix colors on the page by layering or washing them, or you can simply draw thick patches of solid color. There are two types to consider: water-soluble and non-water-soluble. Both types are made with the same pigmentation, but with different binders.

Water-soluble pencils tend to be lower in intensity or brightness than non-water-soluble ones. They can be used for writing and drawing, and can also be stroked onto a page to create layers of color. One interesting option is to turn these layers into washes by brushing them with a wet brush, or stroking on more color to leave texture and stroke marks on top of the washes.

Non-water-soluble or waxy colored pencils tend to be more vibrant and intense than the water-soluble kind. They're somewhat transparent, so they can be layered to produce an infinite number of subtle mixes. Contrary to what many technical manuals say, non-water-soluble colored pencils can be lightened and even erased completely.

GWEN DIEHN *Italy Journal,* **2007**
6 x 7 x 1 inches (15.2 x 17.8 x 2.5 cm); Sewn on Tapes binding laced into a flexible cover with fold-over and tie, leather with Israeli goat vellum tapes; pen

pen and ink

To do so, make a small loop of masking tape, with the sticky side facing out. Wrap the loop around your finger; then tap the colored pencil marks with the sticky side of the tape loop. Depending on how long you tap, you can significantly lighten and even completely remove colored pencil marks from most papers, without damaging the surface of the paper.

Turn waxy colored pencil markings into washes by brushing mineral spirits over colored areas. You can then draw back over the resulting wash, leaving textural strokes.

Waxy colored pencil sometimes rubs off onto the facing page of a journal. To minimize the chance of this happening, gently rub a wadded-up piece of waxed paper over the surface of the page. In extreme cases, interleaf the page with a sheet of waxed paper, cut to size.

Crayons are versatile tools, since you can both draw with them and use them for rubbings. Buy them in an art supply store, where you will find lush, highly pigmented crayons, a far cry from the waxy ones children use.

Watercolors are pigments ground with water and a weak adhesive binder such as gum Arabic. As the water evaporates from the page, a delicate film of pigment remains. Some watercolors include opacifiers such as chalk. This opaque paint is called *gouache*. Watercolors are more transparent

GWEN DIEHN AND JACOB DIEHN *Friday Adventures Journal,* 2009
4 x 6 x ½ inches (10.2 x 15.2 x 1.3 cm); purchased book; pen, pencil, watercolor

MEGAN STONE *Warning,* 2004
8 x 11 inches (20.3 x 27.9 cm); handmade Coptic book, Davey board, paper, thread; collage, ink, poured fluid acrylic PHOTO BY ARTIST

than gouache; use white gouache to add highlights to watercolor paintings and to turn any watercolor into a pastel version of itself. Both types are water-soluble and dry quickly with no surface stickiness; the two mix well with each other.

Buy individual tubes or cakes of the best paints you can afford. A good starter palette

includes new gamboge yellow, cadmium red medium, permanent rose, ultramarine blue, cobalt blue, raw sienna, burnt sienna, burnt umber, and raw umber. You'll need very little highly pigmented paint to change a color, so go slowly when you're mixing colors. Always begin with the lighter hue and gradually add the darker one.

stencils and stamps

Stencils and stamps can be used to repeat a design on your page or to make grids, lines, and headings.

Acrylic mediums are polymer-based products that are used to thin acrylic paints, which imparts a different gloss or matte finish to the work. Acrylic matte medium is the key ingredient for making book cover encrustations (page 58). Acrylics are very weak adhesives; you shouldn't use them for collage or other jobs that require a stronger adhesive.

Absorbent ground is an acrylic product you can use to partially block out text or images you want to work on top of. Originally made to create a paper-like surface on top of non-porous surfaces such as plastic, copper, or glass, absorbent ground is fairly opaque. It dries to a porous, paper-like surface. You can use it to block out or lighten print on a page you're working on. The surface is not as good for watercolor as paper, but it's worth experimenting with. Absorbent ground can also create an interesting surface if you apply a thick coat and then engrave it with a sharp pencil point when it's almost dry.

Page-Building Techniques

Here are some ideas for getting started in the foregoing mediums. A journal is the perfect place to practice these techniques, since your purpose is to record, explore, focus, and note the passing scene. You are the only audience, so the pressure is off.

Drawing

When you draw in a journal, the goal is to focus, clear the mind, and really see what is before you. A drawing can evoke memories with great depth, breadth, and sensory detail.

Based on many years of teaching drawing, I'm convinced that everyone can learn to draw. To get started, simply ask yourself these questions:

What, in fact, do I see? What is its general shape? What does this shape remind me of? How much of it do I want to include in the drawing?

How wide is it compared to its height? How many of its widths equal its height? How big is this part compared to that part? If the "it" is a scene, such as the field in front of your house on a snowy morning, consider what you want to include in the drawing. For example: "The field is twice as wide as it is tall, and the row of trees to the left goes halfway up the side. There is no sky showing, just the bottom of the row of trees at the far end of the field."

Is this part a true horizontal or vertical? If not, how far off the vertical or horizontal is it?

If I dropped a plumb line (a string with a weight tied to the end) from any one point, what would it hit lower down? If I ran a straight horizontal, such as a laser pointer, from the same point, what would it intersect on its journey across?

DO IT YOURSELF

When you're ready to draw something, try this:

1. Hold a pencil or a straight stick at least 6 inches (15 cm) long in one hand, with your arm fully extended in front of you. (You need to keep the relative distance between the object, your eye, and the stick the same throughout the measuring; if you bend your elbow, the distance between your eye and the stick will change, throwing everything off.)

2. Holding the stick in a vertical position, with your elbow straight, close one eye. Place the tip of the stick so that it appears to touch the top edge of the object; then place your thumbnail at the place on the stick where the bottom edge of the object appears to touch the stick. Holding this unit of measurement and keeping your elbow

straight, turn the stick to a horizontal position and count how many of these units fit across the width of the object.

3. To determine how far off the horizontal or vertical an edge or line is, hold the stick perfectly horizontally beneath the edge (or vertically beside it), close one eye, and estimate how much the edge drops below or rises above the horizontal or veers from the vertical.

4. To improvise a plumb line or a straight horizontal, hold the stick horizontally or vertically. Notice what lies directly below, above, or to the left or right of the starting point.

With practice, you'll get good at estimating measurements and comparisons, and you won't need to actually measure so often. But even after years of practice you may say, "This looks funny. Something's off." That's when you'll grab a pencil to measure and compare so you can quickly fix things.

Of course there is more than this to drawing, but these few questions will get you started and will serve you well no matter what else you learn. The real key to learning is practice.

Watercolor Painting

If you want to use watercolor to paint in a realistic style, it's good to imagine you're drawing in color. Start by using a pencil to measure (see page 62) and then lightly sketch the overall dimensions of the scene or object.

GWEN DIEHN *Italy Journal,* 2007
6 x 7 x 1 inches (15.2 x 17.8 x 2.5 cm); Sewn on Tapes binding laced into a flexible cover with fold-over and tie; leather with Israeli goat vellum tapes; pen, watercolor, gouache, absorbent ground

KERSTIN VOGDES *Costa Rica/Nicaragua Journal,* 2008
6 x 6 inches (15.2 x 15.2 cm); soft corrugated paper cover with Multiple Pamphlets sewn in; watercolors, pen, and ink

Next, remember these two things:
1) If you paint over wet paint, your marks will be fuzzy and diffused. If you want crisp definition, wait for the paint to dry completely before painting over or next to it. 2) Always start with the general shape and the lightest color, and then move gradually to the particular details and the darker colors.

ONE EXAMPLE

To paint a small building that I can see across a field, I use a pencil to find the relationship of the building's height to its width. I very lightly sketch in a rectangle to reflect that relationship. I also make marks to indicate where the door is in relation to the chimney, how high the roof is relative to the height of the wall, and other fundamental details. These should be very light, map-like marks. Don't spend time making careful drawings.

Next, I mix up a light color that seems to underlie all the other colors of the building—for example, a pale yellow brown. I brush a diluted coat of this over the rectangles and roofs and let it dry completely.

ADD LAYERS

While the paint dries, I analyze the scene to determine the next darker color on the building. I mix that color, maybe pale lavender, and brush it all over the building *except* in those places where I want the pale yellow brown first coat to show. (If I wanted the second color to blend with the first color, I would brush it on while the first color was still wet.)

While the second color dries, I determine the next darker color, and so on, until I have painted the smallest, darkest details, and

the building is complete. I'm very careful to let the paint dry before I paint the smallest details, as any dampness of the surface will blur what should be crisp, clean marks.

Layered painting like this can be done with any subject matter. You'll gain skill in mixing colors and deciding exactly where to place them, as well as knowing when to leave the underlying color showing through. It's best to wait to use the darkest colors until the very end and then only in those places where the subject is truly that dark.

Using Crayons

In addition to basic wax crayons, art supply stores sell water-soluble crayons, which work something like water-soluble colored pencils. They also sell highly pigmented, intensely colored art crayons (Caran d'Ache is one excellent brand). You can use all of these kinds of crayons to add visual elements to a page.

You can also use the wax kind (non-water-soluble) for the process of crayon resist. First, draw a shape or shapes with a light-colored wax crayon. Then brush watercolor washes over the shape and its background. The watercolor will adhere only to the non-waxy areas of the paper, yielding an interesting surface that resembles batik.

Water-soluble crayons work just like water-soluble colored pencils, but they have thicker points. They also deposit a heavier layer of pigment onto the paper and when they are brushed over with plain water, the resulting surface is somewhat grainy, which adds an interesting texture.

Poured Acrylics

Acrylics are a popular medium for painting in journals. *Fluid acrylics* are better than the regular, heavy-bodied acrylics because they're non-sticky when they dry and they're more highly pigmented.

In addition to painting, you can use fluid acrylics to make interesting page backgrounds, endpapers, and even cover papers by diluting and pouring them randomly on paper. You can paint over this background with watercolors or write with ink; the dried acrylic shapes won't dislodge. Ideally, you should pour the background on unbound sheets of paper, but it's possible to work on pages that you've already bound. For this process, I recommend using Arches cover or text, Velata, and Niddigen paper because they dry flat.

WENDY HALE DAVIS *Fruition*, 2009
8½ x 13¾ inches (21.6 x 35 cm); ink, Caran d'Ache NeoColor 11 crayons, Pentel brush pen, stickers on Hahnemühle Schiller paper PHOTO BY WENDY OGLE

SUSAN GRIESMAIER *Car Journal*, 2006
5 x 7 x 1½ inches (12.7 x 17.8 x 3.8 cm); cloth-bound and stitched binding
made by Patricia John; colored pens and pencils, photos, stickers, collage

WHAT YOU NEED

*A few bottles of fluid acrylics (Golden brand is
the most highly pigmented and transparent)*

*Empty plastic water or soda bottles with a hole
punched in the screw top with an awl—
one for each color*

*Blotter paper (from an art supply store) or, in a
pinch, old newspapers (not the shiny inserts)*

*Large plastic sheet or a plastic garbage
bag cut open to form a sheet*

Medium- to heavy-weight paper

WHAT YOU DO

1. Mix a few drops of fluid acrylic into a
couple of inches (or centimeters) of water
in a bottle. Shake well. Test the mixture on
scrap paper, and if the color is too light, add
a few more drops of paint. If it's too heavy
or dark, add some water and mix again.

2. Lay the sheets of paper on the plastic.
Drip, squirt, or pour the watery paint onto
the paper. Use the blotter to absorb it in
places; tip the page to accelerate a drip; roll
the sheet over on itself to self-blot; push
the paint with your fingers or a sponge or
a feather or a brush—do whatever it takes
to make a sheet of color and shapes that
pleases you. Just play! You can add more
paint and different colors, blotting as you go.

3. If the pages are already bound into a
book, put blotter paper between the sheets
you're pouring onto and the pages beneath
them. Then proceed as in step 2. You can
also fold facing pages over onto each other
to form inkblot-like shapes.

4. When you have the effect you like, turn
the pages over and do the other sides. When
both sides are done, hang the sheets up to
dry, using a clothespin in one corner. You
can also drape them over a towel rack or
lay them on an oven rack or drying rack. If
your pages are in a book, just leave the book
open until the paint dries. This process is
slower if the pages are bound, as you can
only do two facing pages at a time.

DANIELLE BAUMGARTNER
My Dream Journal, 2005
3¼ x 5¾ x 1 inches (8.3 x 14.6 x 2.5 cm);
encrusted cover, poured acrylic, Arches
Cover paper

GWEN DIEHN *Palazzone Wedding Planning Journal,* **2005**
5 x 7 x 1 inches (12.7 x 17.8 x 2.5 cm); watercolor, gouache, acrylic absorbent ground, pen, rubber stamp letters on handmade paper; Sewn on Tapes journal with encrusted cover

Stamps & Relief Prints

Sometimes you just can't find paper with lines in the right places or the right distance apart for your particular journal practice. Perhaps you need grid paper for a calendar or chart. Or you might want to stamp some words in your journal to create titles, labels, and occasional phrases. You probably can find what you need in the rubber stamp department of a craft supply store, and it's easy to modify these stamps to fit your purpose.

For instance, if you buy rubber stamps designed to print ruled lines, you can adjust them so they'll give you exactly the lines you want; simply use a mat knife to cut away every other line to increase the spacing between lines. Or you can arrange two stamps on a clear base (also sold in the stamp department) so that the resulting block of lines is what you need to fill the desired portion of each page with lines.

You can also find stamps with calendar grids. To adjust the stamp to your needs, cut off any elements of the stamp that you don't want with a mat knife, or cut notches into all of the lines at regular intervals to turn them from solid lines to dotted lines.

You can carve your own stamps. You can find blank rubber at an art supply store, but you can also use other materials. Plastic or rubber erasers work very well, as do corks, or even foam earplugs. Here are directions for making a stamp out of an eraser or cork.

WHAT YOU NEED

Graphite pencil

Scrap of paper

Rubber eraser or cork

Mat knife and linoleum carving tools (available at art or craft supply stores)

Pen

Sandpaper

Stamp pad

WHAT YOU DO

1. If you're using an eraser, draw the shape or word you want to carve into your eraser onto a piece of scrap paper with a graphite pencil. (For corks, skip to step 3.)

2. Turn the paper over onto the eraser, with the graphite facing down, and rub the back of the paper with your fingernail. The graphite image will transfer onto the eraser. Notice that this image will be in reverse (a mirror image), which is good, because when you use the finished stamp to print, the image will reverse back to the right side.

3. If you're using a cork, you'll have to first trim away a thin slice off the cork's end with the mat knife and sand it to make a perfectly flat carving surface. The areas in relief must be even or they will not pick up ink smoothly from the stamp pad.

4. Draw the design in non-ballpoint pen.

5. Use a mat knife and linoleum carving tools to carve away the background, leaving the area you want to print standing in relief.

Your stamp prints can be used alone, in borders, or to design entire backgrounds or page surfaces.

Collage

At the heart of many journals are scraps—the ephemera of a journey, an experience, a project, or simply daily life. These include theater tickets, receipts, napkin sketches, wrapping paper, bits of handwriting, sugar packets, labels, magazine clippings, postage stamps, fortune cookie fortunes.

Use your own collection as the basis for designs, in patterns, and as the starting point of drawings. You can cut photographs of gardens from different magazine pages and assemble them into a composite that serves as a plan for new landscaping (page 28). Or cut samples of lettering in foreign languages and combine them with other samples to make backgrounds for pages about travel to places where everything is different.

COLLAGE IN A JOURNAL

Attach collage elements to pages with PVA, YES, or glue stick. Masking tape doesn't last very long and cellophane tape never completely dries, so it's best not to use these. Keep in mind that heavily collaged pages fatten the foredge of a book. You'll need to compensate for the extra bulk by removing a page or two immediately in front of the collaged page.

If some items are too bulky to attach to the page itself, make color copies or scans of them and attach these to your journal pages. Pressed leaves and flowers can be kept in envelopes or can be protected by sealing them under a layer of matte polymer varnish. The varnish will protect natural materials and at the same time attach them to the paper. It's important to use polymer varnish and not polymer medium for this job, as varnish dries hard while medium stays sticky even when dry.

COLLAGE TO BEGIN A DRAWING

Collage can be a low-risk way to start a drawing. First, attach one of your pieces of ephemera to a page. Now use a pencil or other drawing tool to extend the piece of collage. Perhaps you will just continue the background color so that it forms a surface on which you will make some notes. Or you might add more hair to a photo of a person, or lengthen a skirt, or add a pair of rainbow-colored wings. You might start out by tearing a photograph in half, gluing down one of the halves, and drawing in the missing half. You might go wild and invent the second half to better express what you're really thinking or feeling when you look at that picture.

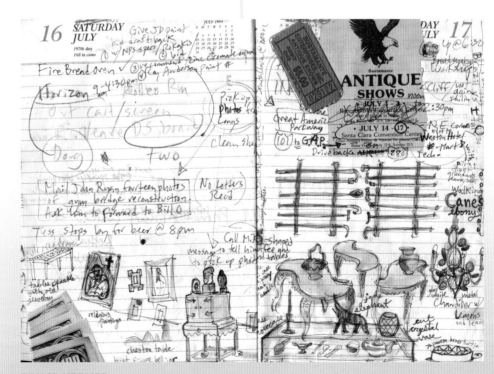

BRUCE KREMER *16–17July94,* **1994**
8 x 11 inches (20.3 x 27.9 cm); combined materials in a diary PHOTO BY ARTIST

Reasons to Write

BY ANN TURKLE

No matter what the primary purpose of a journal may be, writing can enhance it. Even the briefest written entry can provide the essential glue to hold a set of journal entries together and keep them accessible and relevant as time passes.

And yet, when confronted with a new journal, many of us have unpleasant flashbacks about failed attempts at keeping daily diaries—all those blank pages can be daunting. What I actually managed to put on my early diary pages became what I like to call "brain in a jar"—a collection of thoughts and feelings devoid of any setting in time, place, or circumstance.

How, then, can we move beyond false starts and stilted or self-conscious prose to a rich reporting of what we see, hear, smell, and feel? The first step is to quiet our ever-critical brain with its endless chatter about our inadequacies. It can be done. The following suggestions and writing prompts have helped me and my students write more freely and with greater enjoyment and satisfaction.

Seeing with Fresh Eyes

I've often noticed that when I travel, I'm more responsive to what happens to me, better able to see it, and more ready to record my impressions and experiences. I love that level of increased awareness, and that's what I want most to bring home from a trip. I call this way of experiencing things "fresh eyes," a heightened responsiveness I now try to apply in every setting and circumstance. I suspect that "fresh eyes" are easy to have when traveling because, as an outsider, I notice things that I tend to ignore in my everyday environment.

For instance, I love the numerals and signs for money in other countries so much that I often peel price tags off things I buy to paste into my journal. I take more time; am more sensitive to the energy around me; notice colors; pay attention to smells; watch people; even notice how my feet feel touching the ground. I listen to strange sounds and accents and the musical qualities of spoken language. I notice tastes too—for better or for worse. And while I'm noticing, I jot down notes—not necessarily full-blown prose, but little lists and fragments, the odd phrase, a comparison to explain a smell or a sound.

Last night in Ireland, I stayed at a bed and breakfast on the edge of a village in the Burren. Today I walked the Green Road (because of the name) between hedges and stone wall to a pasture, where I watched dogs work the sheep that rushed in front of them like dirty clouds in a storm wind. When sheep and dogs disappeared over the crest of a hill, I stood wishing them back. Then I heard a sound so out of place, I could not believe my ears. I waited and listened again. A cuckoo. A real live cuckoo.

Another writing prompt I use is to ask myself the question: "Could I live here?" That question allows me to blend what is in front of me with musings about a future, one I might never have imagined before. It all goes on the page. On my first trip to Europe, I traveled by sleeper car from Sochi (in the then-Soviet Union) along the Black Sea toward Tbilisi, now in the Georgian Republic. I wrote the following entry one morning:

A rockslide has delayed our train. While the rocks are being removed and the track repaired, I am looking out at a little white house on the edge of the sea. The family sits and eats at a table under an arbor. The sun sparkles off the water, there are flowers, and the leaves of the arbor tremble in a breeze. A thought occurred to me: I could live here. Other lives are possible. I could live here and be happy.

Provide Context

As we make a sketch, record an event, or jot down instructions, we think that there's no way we'll forget when, where, why, or with whom we had this experience. But we often do. Failing to give a journal event its living context may be frustrating when we revisit the entry. Giving each entry a context makes it richer and, most importantly, sharpens our focus as we experience what we're recording.

At a minimum, jot down when and where you've made a drawing, taken a picture, or written an entry. Other contextual notes can provide important orientation. Mention the presence of friends and family members who

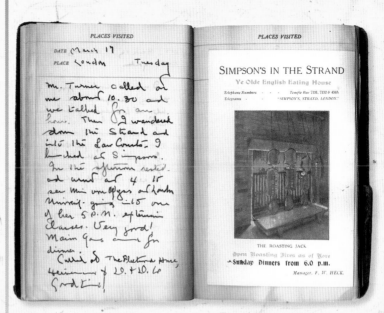

ELLEN EDDY SHAW *Personal travel notes of London and insert of restaurant advertisement in purchased travel diary,* **1931**
Ellen Eddy Shaw Papers, Special Collections, Brooklyn Botanic Garden Library

influenced the direction and urgency of your writing. It's significant to me when I read, *Heather asked me to explain… or Ian told me a story about his work at school that made me think…*

Some historical context is also useful, as my memoir students reminded me. *We lived on a dirt road that became impassable during the heaviest snows and in mud season,* one writer tells her readers. Another explains, *Our father made sure my sisters and I each had a dime to call home when he dropped us off at the movie theatre. (There were no cell phones.)*

When I reread my journal, I often discover the need for added context, which I then jot down in the margins, for example noting that an entry was made at a writing conference in San Antonio or as I was packing for the big move from North Carolina back to Vermont. Context adds another dimension to what I record.

Another contextual element can be the commonplace events surrounding larger projects. While my ultimate purpose in the journal may be to write a short explanatory essay about my garden or my mother's handmade dolls, I prime the writing pump by making a quick observation about how I'm spending my day. *Finished painting the kitchen. All yellow now and glorious in the afternoon sun. Encourages me to cook.* Or: *Sump pump on the fritz again. Hope it stops raining soon!* In retrospect, these observations about ordinary moments may trump the purposeful projects we planned when witnessing our lives.

Using Graphic Prompts

Another tactic I use to facilitate writing is to divide a page into two vertical columns. I then use the columns for a variety of purposes. For example, imagine you're keeping a journal about your move to a new city. Try writing the facts of your first week there on one side, and then write how you felt about each part of the week on the other side. Describe a new experience on one side and what that experience reminded you of from your past on the other side. Write a conversation that you had on one side and what you didn't say but wish you had said on the other side. Make a plan on one side; make a completely different plan on the other side. Write the pros of a decision on one side and the cons on the other. This approach can open the door to writing no matter what kind of journal you're keeping.

Another kind of graphic prompt is to vary your handwriting: if you usually write in cursive, try printing. Use different colors of pens; write on top of and around visuals.

Paying Attention

Sometimes we have many little free moments in our day. We wait at a stoplight, in a checkout line, for our Internet connection, or on the telephone. These "in-between" moments can leave us tapping our toes in impatience, but they can also allow us to turn with pen in hand to a small notebook kept close at hand.

Gradually, this practice can yield great results. You'll learn to pay attention and be aware to what's going on around you, not just what's going on in your head. You'll get comfortable writing about a lot of different things. Your little notebook can go many places your larger journal might not easily fit, so it won't be quite so obvious that you're using it in public.

Several of the journal designs in this book include little "piggyback" collector journals that tuck inside the larger journal. You might copy some of your short notes into entries in your bigger journal, or the little collector journal may serve as a repository of ideas for future reference.

Make Lists, Describe, Witness, Listen & Collect

Lists are liberating. They're much easier to generate than carefully constructed sentences, and they give us an opportunity to discover patterns, similarities, and differences. For instance, in your garden journal, list every flower blooming today. Record the names of the tree species in your yard. Look over your lists and try to determine patterns that evolve. Use descriptive language to record your observations. For example, one morning I came upon a box turtle in my yard and I wrote: *About the size of a large coffee cup, she sat between the broccoli and the tomato plants in the garden. She looked up at me with gold eyes, perfectly coordinated with the gold and greenish brown of her shell.*

As you people-watch, record the actions of those you observe. Sitting on a park bench one day, I noticed four children running through a puddle left by a recent rainstorm and I wrote: *First they ran keeping their feet low to create a wake, then took huge steps, stomping up the biggest splash possible, and finally they ran and slid. They took turns initiating the action, almost the way members of a jazz ensemble take turns improvising.*

When you write about something specific that you're observing or experiencing, you'll find that your "blocks" about writing have been lifted. You may discover that you're a pretty good writer, even though the quality of the writing is not the "point" of the journal.

Eavesdrop, record dialogue, and listen to what your surroundings tell you. I lived for two years on a corner in a residential neighborhood in Tallahassee, Florida. Gradually, I realized I could describe that neighborhood, the time of day, the season, and the weather just by listening. The bus service to my corner started at 7:00 a.m. and ended in the early evening, each pass punctuated by the distinctive squeal of brakes. The magnolia tree outside my window dropped its leaves with a sound almost as decisive as smashing plates. How would you describe the distinctive qualities of your neighborhood by sound? And how could you make those sounds visible?

Revisiting the Journals

I'm perplexed that many avid journal keepers don't use or refer to them once they're completed. One writing exercise I routinely practice is what I call "carrying forward." Periodically, I pick up an old journal and read through it. I may intend to mine a journal for specific information (How much did it cost to rent the lake cottage in 2007?) or just see what I was paying attention to this time last year. Inevitably I find an observation, a question, or a quote that deserves repeating in my current journal. I've evolved a system of journal tags that indicate the date span each covers, and I number the pages so I can make easy references. I return to my existing journals when I'm bored, tired, or lack focus. They energize me and give me a new sense of purpose and direction.

My journals, enriched and enlivened with writing, are a sort of how-to book, an intimate instruction manual that allows me to observe the patterns of my life. As the author Edward Said observed:

"Regard experiences as if they were about to disappear: What is it about them that anchors or roots them in reality? What would you save of them? What would you give up, what would you recover? To answer such questions you must have the independence and detachment of someone whose homeland is 'sweet,' but whose actual condition makes it impossible to recapture the sweetness… Seeing 'the entire world as a foreign land' makes possible originality of vision." Said, Edward. (*Reflections on Exile and Other Essays*; Harvard University Press, 2002.)

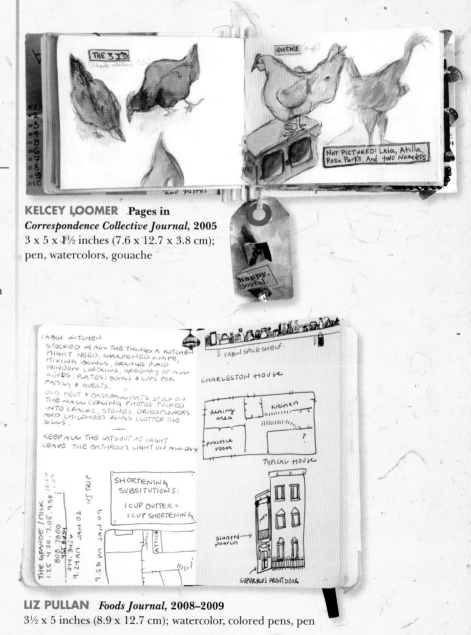

KELCEY LOOMER Pages in
***Correspondence Collective Journal*, 2005**
3 x 5 x 1½ inches (7.6 x 12.7 x 3.8 cm);
pen, watercolors, gouache

LIZ PULLAN *Foods Journal*, **2008–2009**
3½ x 5 inches (8.9 x 12.7 cm); watercolor, colored pens, pen

CHAPTER 4

16 bookbinding instructions

Before you make any of these book forms, be sure to design your journal by completing the Design Inventory in Chapter One. Then turn to the *Choose Your Own Bookbinding Adventure* booklet stored in the envelope inside the front cover and follow the prompts. This design process will reveal which of these 16 book forms best suits the purpose of your journal.

The 16 book forms range from very easy pamphlets and ledger books to more intricate and surprising Australian books, from flexible notebooks that you can roll up and slip into your back pocket to elegant, satin-covered full-case bindings. Browse through this chapter to see other possibilities and get ideas for future projects.

Pamphlet

The Pamphlet is a basic book form that makes an ideal piggyback. It is essentially a single signature sewn through its fold. When you construct a Pamphlet, you often sew the cover right along with the single signature, as in the directions below, but you can choose to glue a Pamphlet to a hard cover (page 147) or to a flexible cover such as a piece of unmounted leather (page 133).

WHAT YOU NEED

Bookbinding Tool Kit (page 47)

Text pages in folios (see Bookbinding Essentials)

Heavy paper for the cover

Scrap paper for the pattern, 2 inches (5.1 cm) x the height of the text pages

Straight needle

1 yard (91.4 cm) of bookbinder's thread

WHAT YOU DO

PREPARING TO SEW

1 Cut or tear the pages to size and fold each one separately, burnishing the fold so the crease is crisp and flat. Nest the folios into each other, forming a single signature (see Bookbinding Essentials).

2 To make the cover, cut or tear the heavy paper so it is ⅛ inch (3 mm) taller and ½ inch (1.3 cm) wider than the unfolded text pages. Fold the cover in half widthwise, and slip the text signature inside (figure 1 on the next page).

3 Using the scrap paper as a pattern, punch three (or any odd number of) holes in both the signature and the cover with the awl and telephone book, as shown in Bookbinding Essentials.

SEWING THE TEXT PAGES AND COVER

4 Thread the needle, but do not tie a knot. You can tie the thread off on the inside or the outside of the book. To tie it off on the inside, insert the needle in the center hole from the inside; to tie it off on the outside, insert the needle into the center hole from the outside. See Bookbinding Essentials for sewing tips.

GWEN DIEHN **Untitled, 2009**
4 x 6 x ¼ inches (10.2 x 15.2 x 1.3 cm);
Pamphlet book with cover fold-ins

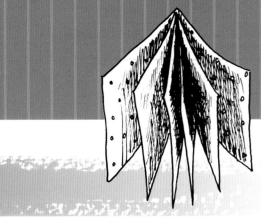

figure 1

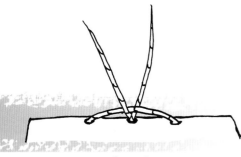

figure 2

figure 3

KONRAD ZOLL *Dancing Palms,* 2005
8¼ x 5½ inches (21 x 14 cm); graphite pencil PHOTO BY ARTIST

5 Pull the thread through, leaving a 4-inch (10.2 cm) tail. Clip or hold the tail so you don't pull it through. Then insert the needle into the next hole, either up or down from the center. Pull gently, parallel to the plane of the book, to tighten the stitch.

6 If your book has three holes, continue with step 7. Otherwise, proceed to the next hole (away from the center), sewing all the holes in that direction. When you reach the last hole, proceed back toward the center.

7 Bring the needle across the center hole and insert it into the first hole on the other side. Tighten the stitch. (If your book has more holes, sew all the holes in that direction and back again.) Then insert the needle back into the center hole and pull the thread through so the thread and the tail are on opposite sides of the long center stitch (figure 2). Tie the thread across the long center stitch (figure 3).

CUSTOMIZING THE COVER

Once you have the basics down, you can easily make a few changes to the cover:

Consider cutting the cover paper a few inches wider (or even twice as wide). By folding in this extra width, you will make the cover sturdier.

Optionally, stitch the top and bottom edges of the cover fold-ins to make pockets inside the covers.

Slip a piece of scrap cardboard between the front cover and the first page to protect the text block. Then cut a window in the cover. Place an illustration or title on the first page, positioned so it shows through the cover window.

Album

The best thing about an Album is how easily you can replace, remove, and add pages. You can also fatten its spine to keep the foredge from splaying open when you add thick elements to the pages. Albums work for single pages and don't require folios, although they can accommodate folios and reverse folios (see Bookbinding Essentials). Although Albums traditionally take a hard cover that doesn't lend itself to being folded back, you can break tradition and make a foldable cover.

WHAT YOU NEED

Bookbinding Tool Kit (page 47)

Text pages (see Bookbinding Essentials)

Strips of paper, 1 inch (2.5 cm) x the height of the text pages

Spine fatteners for selected text pages (optional)

2 covers (see page 125 for directions)

2 C-clamps

4 pieces of stiff cardboard or mat board, each about 1½ inches (3.8 cm) square

Scrap wood as big as or bigger than the closed book

Electric or hand drill with a ¼-inch (6 mm) bit

2 screw posts, as long as the book is thick

SUSAN AMELIA STRYKER
Memory and Fellowship Book, 1910
17 x 12⅜ x 3 inches (43.2 x 31.5 x 7.6 cm);
bookcloth-covered Album book; photographs, ink

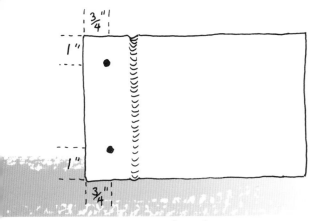

figure 1

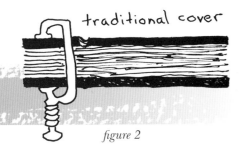

traditional cover

figure 2

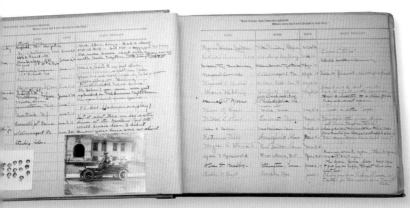

SUSAN AMELIA STRYKER *Memory and Fellowship Book,* **1910**
17 x 12⅜ x 3 inches (43.2 x 31.5 x 7.6 cm); Album book; photographs, ink

WHAT YOU DO

1 Assemble all the pages. To accommodate fold-out pages or thick elements added to the pages, insert a spine fattener or stub before these pages (see Bookbinding Essentials).

2 Place the resulting text block between the two covers. The covers, either traditional or fold-back, should already be covered with cloth, paper, or leather and should have end papers glued in place.

3 Pencil mark two places about ¾ inch (1.9 cm) in from the spine edge where you will insert the screw posts (figure 1). Leave at least 1 inch (2.5 cm) above and below each point. If your book is very large, leave even more space to balance the design.

4 Use the C-clamps to hold the cover and text block tightly together (figure 2). Stick a piece of stiff cardboard under each contact point of the C-clamps to avoid denting or marking the covers.

5 Lay the book on top of the scrap wood. Carefully drill two holes at the pencil marks, keeping the drill bit straight up so the holes go straight down. Reverse the drill to remove the bit from the covers when you've reached the bottom.

6 Brush off any paper crumbs and waste from the cover. Place the screw posts into the holes and tighten the screws.

Ledger

A very old Japanese binding, the Ledger was originally used for account books. The text pages of traditional Ledger books were composed of sheets of thin paper folded on the foredge to create double-thick sheets that prevented ink from bleeding through. The foredge folds, when painted straight across the edges, formed attractive designs visible when the books were closed.

ERIN JOHNSON *Cake*, 2007
2½ x 4 inches (6.4 x 10.2 cm); paper with stiff cloth over-cover COLLECTION OF THE AUTHOR

WHAT YOU NEED

Bookbinding Tool Kit (page 47)

Text pages, either single sheets or with foredge folds (see Bookbinding Essentials)

Page stubs (see Bookbinding Essentials) to add pages, envelopes, etc.

2 covers (see page 127)

Heavy-duty clip (see figure 2 on the next page)

Scrap wood for drilling or punching into

Drill with a ¹⁄₁₆- or ⅛-inch (1.6 or 3 mm) drill bit (optional)

Heavy, 3-ply bookbinder's thread

Straight needle

WHAT YOU DO

1 Assemble the pages between the two covers. Be sure to include any stubs you'll need. Mark the places for drilling two cover holes, which must be at least ½ inch (1.3 cm) from any edge to avoid tearing (figure 1).

figure 1

figure 2

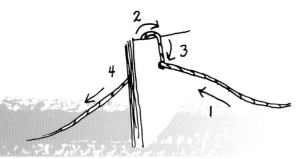

figure 3

figure 4

figure 5

2 Clamp the pages and covers together to keep them from moving (figure 2). Place the book on the scrap wood and use either the drill or the awl to drill or punch through all pages and both covers at one time.

3 Thread the needle with about 1 yard (91.4 cm) of thread. Insert the needle into either hole and pull the thread through, leaving a tail around 5 inches (12.7 cm) long.

4 Lap the side of the book and return the needle through the same hole (figure 3).

5 Lap the spine and tie the thread to the tail, making both cut ends around 5 inches (12.7 cm) long (figure 4). Repeat steps 3, 4, and 5 for the other hole.

6 Optionally, tie the tails together, fray their ends, or thread beads onto them. See figure 5.

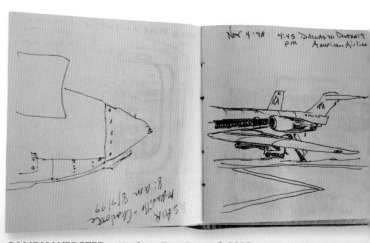

SANDY WEBSTER *Airplane Fear Journal*, 2009
4 x 4 inches (10.2 x 10.2 cm); pen PHOTO BY ARTIST

Spiral Binding

Spiral binding opens and stays flat while allowing you to fold pages completely around to the back of the book. Although it's easy to find different sizes, shapes, and colors of spiral-bound books to use as journals, rarely can you find one that has the special kind of paper you might need for a particular project. If you want the convenience of this binding combined with the paper you like, consider making your own spiral-bound book. Once you put together all the ingredients, you can have it bound at an office supply store or at a quick printer's shop.

WHAT YOU NEED

Bookbinding Tool Kit (page 47)

Single, unfolded pages cut to size (see Page Note)

2 pieces of cover material (see Cover Note)

Rubber stamp of horizontal lines and a stamp pad (optional)

Paper for a pocket (optional)

Paste wax (optional)

BARBARA ROTH
Cheeze-It Journal, **2008**
6 x 8 inches (15.2 x 20.3 cm);
laminated cracker box, 93#
Aquabee watercolor paper, pastel
paper, drawing paper, card stock
PHOTO BY ARTIST

Page Note: You might also consider using envelopes, maps, and various other papers (such as tracing paper, watercolor paper, and grid paper). You can also bind in some stubs or spine fatteners (see Bookbinding Essentials) so that you can add other kinds of paper or found items later. It's even possible to bind in a map or a foldout page as long as you leave ¾ inch (1.9 cm) on the left edge for the binding.

Cover Note: Slightly flexible boards (such as mat board, recycled cartoons and boxes, or cover-weight paper) work best. Check with the bindery workers (at the office supply or quick printer's shop) to find out how heavy the cover can be and still go through their machinery. You can paint, print, or collage on your cover boards, or you can use them as is. If you are using colored mat board, consider treating the outside surface with a cold wax medium (available in art supply stores) or any light paste wax to make the cover water-resistant, to deepen the color, and to enrich the surface.

figure 1

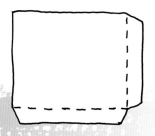

figure 2

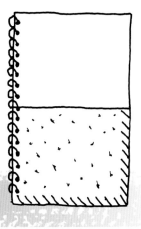

figure 3

WHAT YOU DO

1 Find an office supply store or a quick printer's shop and ask if they do spiral binding. Most places offer comb binding, wire and plastic spiral binding, as well as either wire or plastic spiral binding and a variety of sizes of combs and spirals ranging from ¼ inch (6 mm) to nearly 1 inch (2.5 cm) in diameter. No job is too small in my experience; it costs very little and often takes less than 30 minutes to have the job done.

2 It's a good idea to show the binder what materials you want bound. Make sure your cover material isn't too heavy for their punching machine. Choose a spiral or comb big enough to handle all of your pages. Most machines can punch only a limited number of pages. Once you have all this information, cut or tear your chosen text pages and cut your selected cover boards (page 49).

3 Take all of your materials to the office supply store or quick printer to be bound. If you want, have them bind a pocket into the front and/or back cover. To make a pocket, cut a piece of paper to the desired pocket size plus a ½-inch (1.3 cm) glue tab along the bottom and outside edge (figure 1). Fold each glue tab under (figure 2). Apply PVA to the exposed side of each glue tab and then press the tabs to the bottom and side of the cover board. When the book is bound, the unglued edge of the pocket is bound with the rest of the book (figure 3).

Multiple Pamphlet

A Multiple Pamphlet consists of two or more pamphlets sewn directly into pleats in the flexible heavy-paper cover. Use this simple binding as a piggyback that you can slip inside a larger journal. For a more substantial book, you may use between four and seven pamphlets. You can glue the book into a hard cover (page 147) or into a flexible leather or cloth cover (page 133). Another option is to sew the book directly into a flexible cover with no pleats between the pamphlets (page 139).

WHAT YOU NEED

Bookbinding Tool Kit (page 47)

2–7 pamphlets (text pages in signatures) (see Bookbinding Essentials)

Pleated cover/concertina (page 92)

Hole-punching pattern

4 paper clips

Straight needle

1 yard (91.4 cm) of thread (for the first signature) and an extra 12 inches (30.5 cm) of thread for each additional signature

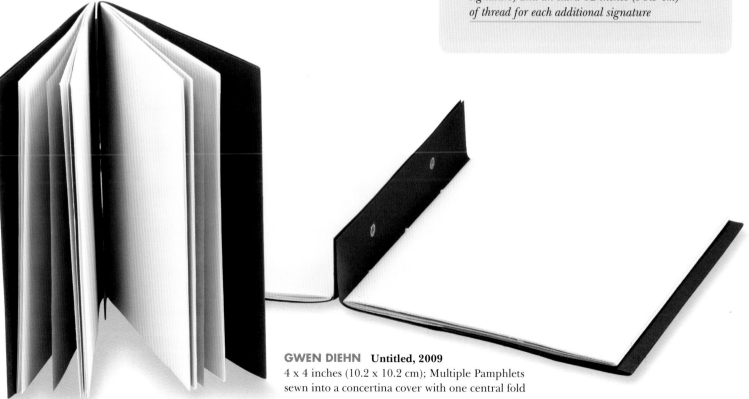

GWEN DIEHN Untitled, 2009
4 x 4 inches (10.2 x 10.2 cm); Multiple Pamphlets
sewn into a concertina cover with one central fold

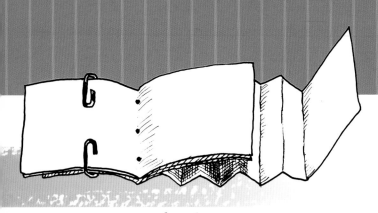

figure 1

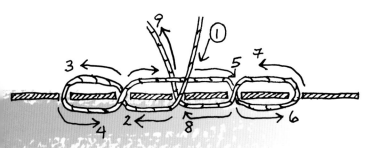

figure 2

GWEN DIEHN **Journal, 2007**
4 x 6 inches (10.2 x 15.2 cm); Multiple Pamphlets
sewn into a leather cover

WHAT YOU DO

1 Nest the first pamphlet into the crease between the cover and first pleat of the concertina. Press the pattern into the center crease of the pamphlet. Place all of these elements into a center crease of the telephone book (see Bookbinding Essentials). Punch holes through the text pages and concertina.

2 Stabilize the pamphlet with paper clips (figure 1). Thread the needle and insert it into the center hole from outside the book. Pull the thread until a 4-inch (10.2 cm) tail remains. Clip the tail under one of the paper clips to keep it in place. See Bookbinding Essentials for sewing tips.

3 Insert the needle into the next hole up or down, gently pulling the thread parallel to the plane of the book until it sits snugly against the crease of the signature.

4 If your book has only three holes, insert the needle into the remaining hole, stretching the thread across the center hole. Proceed to step 6.

5 If your book has more than three holes, continue sewing as in step 3 until you reach the end of the row of holes in that direction. Now sew back toward the center, skipping over the center hole when you come to it. Continue sewing in the other direction until you are back at the center hole (figure 2).

6 Insert the needle from inside the pamphlet into the center hole (which has the tail already coming out of it). Be sure the thread and the tail are on opposite sides of the long center stitch (figure 2 again).

7 Tie off the book as in figure 3, but do not cut the thread. Insert the still-threaded needle into the center hole of the next signature from the outside.

8 To attach the remaining pamphlets, repeat steps 3 to 7, punching and sewing each one before proceeding to the next.

9 If the book has more than two or three pamphlets, you need to link the top and bottom rows of stitching to each other, just as the center rows are naturally linked. After you tie off the last pamphlet, cut the thread. Then anchor the thread to the first pamphlet's top row of stitches by first tying the thread on, inside the first pamphlet (figure 4).

10 Insert the needle through the hole from the inside, and make a loop stitch through the top stitch of the next pamphlet (figure 5). Continue linking the stitches in this manner until all pamphlets are linked together at the top. Insert the needle into the last hole, and tie off the book on the inside (see Bookbinding Essentials).

11 Repeat steps 9 and 10 for the bottom row of stitches, anchoring the thread to the inside of the bottom stitch in the first pamphlet (figure 4 again).

12 If you want to customize the cover, see page 54.

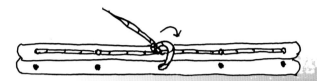

figure 3

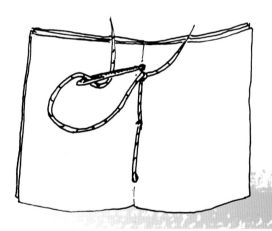

figure 4

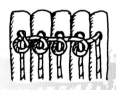

figure 5

Flat-Style Australian Reversed Piano Hinge

Like the Round-Style Hinge, this binding allows you to easily remove and replace every page. The hinge in *this* style is sleek and flat. If you want to turn pages 360°, just as you can in a spiral bound book, see the directions for the Round-Style Australian Reversed Piano Hinge (page 87).

WHAT YOU NEED

Bookbinding Tool Kit (page 47)

Paper for text pages in folios (see Bookbinding Essentials)

Concertina with enough pleats to accommodate all the folios in the book

Scrap paper, 2 inches (5.1 cm) x the height of the text pages

Paper for the hinge pins, the same weight as the concertina

GWEN DIEHN *Brasstown Pigments*, 2009
4½ x 6½ x 2 inches (11.4 x 16.5 x 5.1 cm); hand-bound Flat-Style Australian Reversed Piano Hinge; watercolor, pen, clay samples

WHAT YOU DO

1 Assemble the text pages in folios (see Bookbinding Essentials). Then plan and make a concertina (page 92) with each pleat 1 inch (2.5 cm) wide (figure 1). The concertina binds the pages together. The length of the concertina pleats depends on the size of the text pages, which must extend at least ¾ inch (1.9 cm) farther on each end than the concertina paper.

In a large book, you can use more than one concertina. For example, in an 8-inch (20.3 cm) high book, you might use two 1-inch (2.5 cm) concertinas with one 2-inch (5.1 cm) concertina between them (figure 2). On the other hand, in a small book—one that's no more than 6 inches (115.2 cm) high—you might use a single 4-inch (10.2 cm) concertina.

2 Make a pattern first. Fold the 2-inch (5.1 cm) wide piece of scrap paper in half lengthwise. Arrange the concertinas next to the fold in the scrap paper pattern corresponding to how you want them in the book. Mark the top and bottom of each concertina (figure 3). Be sure no mark comes any closer than ¾ inch (1.9 cm) from any edge or any other mark. Use the awl to punch a hole in the crease of the pattern paper at each mark.

3 Lay the pattern paper in the crease of each folio in turn. Cut through the pattern from hole to hole, exactly in the fold of each folio where you want to insert the concertina pleat(s). If you're using multiple concertinas, position the cuts relative to each other, according to

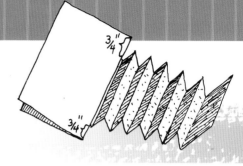

figure 1

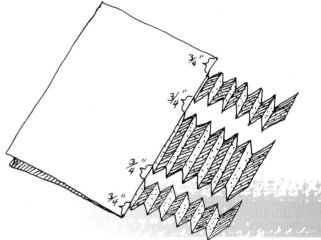

figure 2

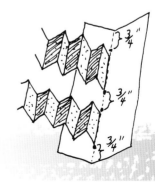

figure 3

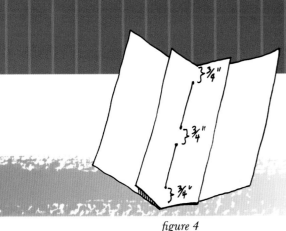

figure 4

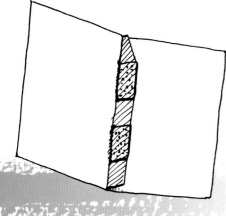

figure 5

figure 6

the pattern. Be sure to leave at least ¾ inch (1.9 cm) of uncut paper between each cut, above the top cut, and below the bottom cut (figure 4). Cutting too close to the edges weakens the paper, making it subject to tearing.

4 Cut the hinge pins the exact height of the text page and about ¹⁄₁₆ inch (1.6 mm) less wide than the concertina pleat(s) so the pleat has enough room to slide into the hinge pin. For example, if your pleat is 1 inch (2.5 cm) wide, make hinge pins about ¹⁵⁄₁₆ inch (2.4 cm) wide. The hinge pins will stick out of the pleats a little since the concertina is a little smaller than the text pages. You need one hinge pin for each page. If you're using multiple concertinas, you still need only one hinge pin per page. The hinge slips through all the concertina pleats in the folio at one time.

5 Pick up the first folio and the first concertina pleat. Carefully slide the pleat into the cut in the fold of the folio. Push the folio down on either side of the pleat to seat the pleat completely in the folio. Now slide a hinge pin through one open end of the pleat. Push it through until it comes out the other end, anchoring the folio to the concertina. If you're using more than one concertina pleat, push the hinge through each pleat in turn. If you have trouble getting the paper hinge pin through the pleat, cut one end at a slant (figure 5).

6 Repeat step 5 for the rest of the concertina pleats and folios (figure 6).

7 To make a cover for your book, refer to the directions for the desired cover. Appropriate covers for this binding style are a hard cover (page 147), flexible cover (page 133), or self cover (page 123). Choose the cover that best fits your plans.

Round-Style Australian Reversed Piano Hinge

Like the Flat-Style Hinge, this binding allows you to easily remove and replace every page. The hinge in this style—made with small sticks, such as bamboo skewers—enables you to turn the pages 360°, as in a spiral bound book. The somewhat bulky hinge fattens the book's spine so you can add elements to the pages while keeping the foredge from splaying open. If you prefer a flat hinge for a sleeker, more compact text block, see the directions for the Flat-Style Australian Reversed Piano Hinge (page 84).

WHAT YOU NEED

Bookbinding Tool Kit (page 47)

Paper for text pages in folios (see Bookbinding Essentials)

Concertina with enough pleats to accommodate all of the folios in the book

Small strip of scrap paper

Material for hinge pins that are relatively even and smooth—such as sticks, twigs, or barbeque skewers between ⅛ and ¼ inch (3 and 6 mm) in diameter

Scrap paper, 2 inches (5.1 cm) x the height of the text pages

GWEN DIEHN *Boat Journal,* **2008**
4 x 6½ x ½ inches (10.2 x 16.5 x 1.3 cm); Round-Style Australian Reversed Piano Hinge with self cover; poured acrylic, watercolor, pen

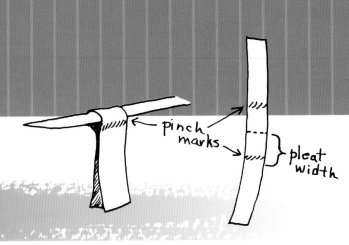

figure 1

figure 2

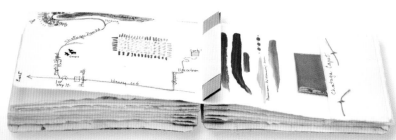

GWEN DIEHN *Brasstown Pigments,* **2009**
4½ x 6½ x 2 inches (11.4 x 16.5 x 5.1 cm); Flat-Style Australian
Reversed Piano hinge; local clay watercolors, pen, pigment sample

WHAT YOU DO

1 Assemble the text pages in folios (see Bookbinding Essentials). Next, plan and make a concertina (page 92). Measure the diameter of the stick hinge pin with the small piece of scrap paper, and make the concertina pleats slightly wider than half the diameter of the stick (figure 1). The height of the concertina depends on the size of the text pages since the concertina binds the pages together.

In a large book, you can use more than one concertina. For example, in an 8-inch (20.3 cm) high book, you might use two 1-inch (2.5 cm) concertinas with one 2-inch (5.1 cm) concertina between them. On the other hand, in a small book—one that's no more than 6 inches (15.2 cm) high—you might use a single 4-inch (10.2 cm) concertina. Figure 2 shows examples of concertinas for different book sizes.

2 Once you have the concertina(s), make a pattern before cutting any of the text pages. Fold the 2-inch-wide (5.1 cm) piece of scrap paper in half lengthwise. Arrange the concertinas next to the fold in the scrap paper pattern corresponding to how you want them in the book. Mark the top and bottom of each concertina (figure 3). Make sure no mark comes any closer than ¾ inch (1.9 cm) from any edge or other mark. Use the awl to punch a small hole in the crease of the pattern paper at each mark.

3 Lay an opened-out folio on the cutting surface, and then align the pattern crease in the folio's crease. Using the pattern as a guide, cut into the fold of the folio from mark to mark. These cuts must be the length of the concertina pleats, positioned exactly where you want to insert them in the folio (figure 4). Repeat this step for all of the folios in the book.

4 Since you're using sticks for hinge pins, cut them a little longer than the length of the text pages. You need one hinge pin for each page. If you are using multiple concertinas, you still need only one hinge pin per page. The hinge slips through all the concertina pleats in the folio at one time and sticks out of the end pleats a little.

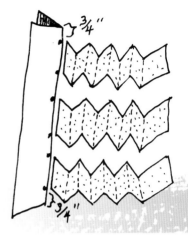

figure 3

5 Pick up the first folio and the first concertina pleat. Carefully slide the pleat(s) into the cut(s) in the fold of the folio. Push the folio down on either side of the pleat to seat the pleat completely in the folio. Now slide a stick hinge pin through one open end of the pleat. Push it through until it comes out the other end, anchoring the folio to the concertina. If you're using more than one concertina pleat, push the stick hinge through each pleat in turn in the same manner until the stick anchors all the pleats in that folio (figure 5). If you have trouble pushing a stick through, cut one end at an angle.

figure 4

6 Repeat step 5 for the rest of the concertina pleats and folios (figure 2 again). You'll enjoy the elegant simplicity with which this binding comes together.

7 When you've bound together all folios, turn to the cover style you want. Appropriate covers for this binding style include a self cover (page 123), a hard cover (page 147), or a flexible glued-in cover (page 133).

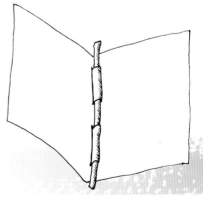

figure 5

Longstitch

ALongstitch binding, as described in this book, has spine openings and strap-like structures that function as sewing tapes. This is an excellent binding to use for making books out of recycled cartons that have interesting designs or that in some way relate to the purpose of the book.

GWEN DIEHN
Travel Journal, **2005**
6 x 4 x 1 inches (15.2 x 10.2 x 2.5 cm); Longstitch binding, recycled hardcover book cover

WHAT YOU NEED

Bookbinding Tool Kit (page 47)

Scrap paper, 2 inches (5.1 cm) x the height of the signatures

Text pages in signatures (see Bookbinding Essentials)

Longstitch cover (page 131)

Heavy, 3-ply bookbinder's thread in a color that complements the design

Straight bookbinder's needle

WHAT YOU DO

1 Using the scrap paper, make a pattern to punch holes in the signatures. Fold the scrap paper in half lengthwise and hold it beside the spine section of the cover. Pencil mark the top and bottom points of each sewing strap on the cover onto the scrap paper. Then add a mark between ¼ and ½ inch (6 and 13 mm) from the top and bottom edges (figure 1).

2 With the pattern, punch holes in the signatures using the awl and telephone book (see Bookbinding Essentials).

3 Pick up the first signature and place it inside the cover. Insert the threaded needle from the outside into the bottom-most hole of the signature. Pull the thread through, leaving a tail about 5 inches (12.7 cm) long. Clip the tail to the cover or hold it to keep it from pulling through.

4 Put the needle into the next hole, from inside the signature to the outside. Pull the thread through and over the first strap in the spine of the cover. Then insert the thread into the next hole, back to the inside of the signature (figure 2).

5 Repeat step 4, sewing over all remaining straps until you finish sewing over the last strap at the top or head of the cover. Come out of the last hole of the signature from the inside and pause.

6 Pick up the second signature and place it right next to the first, already-sewn signature. Put the needle, from the outside, into the top hole of the second signature, which should be just across from the top hole of the first signature.

7 Pull the thread through, and then put the needle into the second hole, from the inside to the outside of the signature. When the needle comes out, pull the thread over the top strap and then put the needle into the hole just under the strap to get back to the inside of the signature.

8 Continue sewing over all the straps. Stop when you reach the bottom of the second signature, just across from the first hole at the bottom of the first signature. This is the hole with the tail hanging out of it. Carefully tie the tail to the thread coming out of the second signature so that you secure the first two signatures. Do not cut the thread, but continue sewing by putting the needle into the first hole of the third signature.

9 Repeat steps 4 and 5. Before you put the needle into the first hole of the next new signature, scoop between the last two signatures (figure 3). This scoop is necessary to tie the signatures together. After the scoop, put

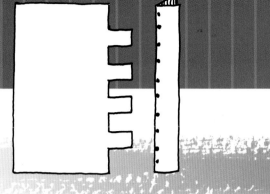

figure 1

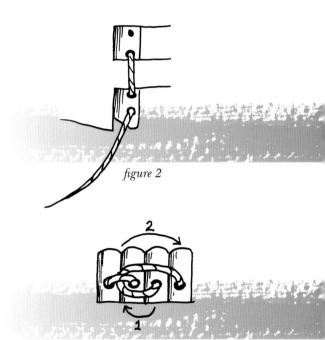

figure 2

figure 3

the needle into the first hole of the new signature and continue sewing. Each time you come to the end of a signature at either end of the book, before you begin on the next signature, do another scoop stitch to tie the signatures together.

10 When you've finished sewing all the signatures, put the needle to the inside of the last signature and tie off the book (see Bookbinding Essentials).

Concertina

n the bookbinding world, a concertina is basically an accordion with shallow folds. A concertina protects the text block in an open-spine binding such as Coptic (page 98). Its folds can also act as stubs for attaching flat inserts. Stubs function as spine fatteners and help keep the book from splaying open should you add thick material to its pages. It's also easy to fold a concertina so some or all of its folds become full-size, double-thick pages that you can use as slipcases or envelopes.

To use a concertina, nest the signatures or folios (see Bookbinding Essentials) into the valley folds. Then sew the signatures plus the concertina fold wrapping together as one unit. You might find it a bit awkward to hold the long, springy concertina while keeping the other pieces in place, so try resting the concertina on the table as you sew. Even if you drop everything on the floor a few times, you'll soon figure out a good system for holding everything. Your efforts will be rewarded in the end.

WHAT YOU NEED

Bookbinding Tool Kit (page 47)

Paper that is equal to or slightly heavier than the chosen text paper

Triangle with a 90° angle

KERSTIN VOGDES *Costa Rica/Nicaragua Journal,* 2008
6 x 6 inches (15.2 x 15.2 cm); corrugated paper cover, Longstitch binding
with concertina, envelope attached to concertina fold; watercolors, pen, ink

WHAT YOU DO

1 Measure the concertina paper according to figure 1. Be sure the grain of the paper (page 49) lies parallel to the folds. If one sheet is not large enough for your needs, lengthen it to the correct size. Refer to the sidebar (page 94) for directions on lengthening the paper.

2 Place the ruler just below the page. Align the triangle with the ruler and then shift it just to the left (or right, if you're left-handed) of the measure of the width of a single text page. Score the paper several times along the upright edge of the triangle with the bone folder. This is the first valley fold.

3 Slide the triangle 1 inch (2.5 cm) to the right and score again. This score marks the first mountain fold. Continue moving and scoring until you've scored every fold. Here is the formula: One score for the first signature, and two scores for each of the remaining signatures (figure 2). For Australian reversed piano hinge books, use this formula: make two scores for each folio (figure 3).

4 If you want to make any full-page-size folds (for a slipcase or envelope), follow this step. After scoring the valley fold just before the large fold you want, move the triangle the width of a text page to the right, and then score the paper. For example, if the text page is 5 inches (12.7 cm) wide, move the triangle that distance before scoring again. Then move the triangle the same distance again and score to complete the large fold. Figure 4 on page 94 shows an example.

5 When you've scored the entire concertina, accordion fold the paper along all the score lines, carefully lining up the bottoms and sides of all the folds (figure 5 on page 94). Burnish all folds with the bone folder.

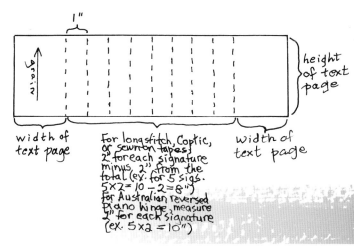

width of text page

For longstitch, Coptic, or sewn on tapes, 2" for each signature minus 2" from the total (ex. for 5 sigs. 5×2=10−2=8"). For Australian reversed piano hinge, measure 2" for each signature (ex. 5×2=10")

width of text page

grain

height of text page

figure 1

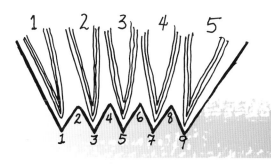

figure 2

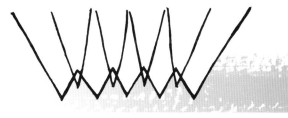

figure 3

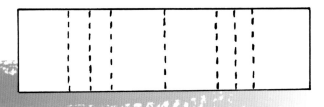

figure 4

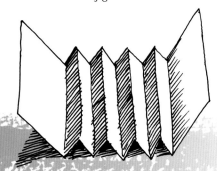

figure 5

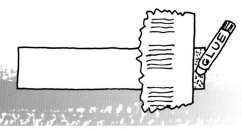

figure 6

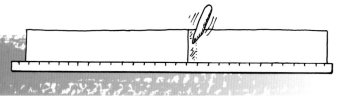

figure 7

LENGTHENING A CONCERTINA PAPER

Sometimes you need to lengthen a piece of paper to make a concertina the desired size. You can easily join two or more pieces of paper together.

1 Cut two or more pieces of concertina paper so that together they measure the desired length for the finished concertina, plus ½ inch (1.3 cm) for each glue tab you need to make. For example, if you have two pieces of paper, and you want to make a concertina that's 12 inches (30.5 cm) long, the paper you have should together measure 13 inches (33 cm) to account for the glue tabs. Be sure the paper's grain is parallel to the folds (the height of the concertina).

2 Lay a piece of scrap paper with at least one straight edge over the right-hand side of the concertina paper, leaving ½ inch (1.3 cm) of the concertina paper extending beyond the straight side of the scrap. Spread a glue stick or YES paste over the ½-inch (1.3 cm) wide section (figure 6).

3 Place the ruler just below the concertina paper. Lay the next piece of concertina paper ½ inch (1.3 cm) over the pasted edge of the first. Line up the bottom of both sheets along the ruler so that they are perfectly square with each other. Burnish the pasted area (figure 7).

4 To add other sheets of paper to obtain the correct length, repeat steps 2 and 3 as needed.

Longstitch with Concertina

A Longstitch binding (page 90) has openings in the spine between the stitches. Adding a concertina to this binding closes the spine somewhat as the concertina paper protects the text pages. You can use the concertina folds themselves as stubs for adding elements, or enlarge the stubs to whole-page size to use as slipcases, envelopes, or double-thick pages.

GWEN DIEHN *Chicken Journal,* **2009**
9 x 7 x 1 inches (22.9 x 17.8 x 2.5 cm); Longstitch with concertina of oiled wire-inlaid paper with flexible leather cover; watercolor, pen, collage, pencil

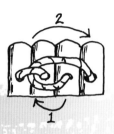

figure 1

figure 2

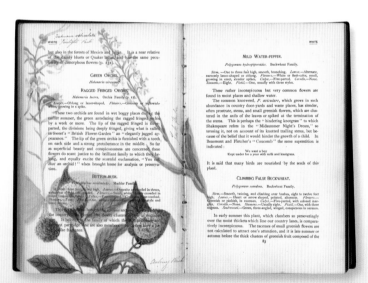

WHAT YOU DO

MAKING AND USING THE PATTERN

1 Make a pattern for punching holes in the concertina and signatures. First, fold the scrap paper in half lengthwise. Place this pattern paper next to the spine of the closed longstitch cover. Figure 1 shows a cover with three sewing straps. If your book is more than 6 inches (15.2 cm) high, consider adding another strap or two. You can have any number of straps, even or odd. You can also vary the strap thickness and the space between them.

2 On the pattern paper, pencil mark a spot for a hole at the top and bottom of each sewing strap. Then add a mark between ¼ and ½ inch (6 and 13 mm) from the top and bottom edges (figure 1 again). Reverse the fold of the pattern so the marks are on the inside crease.

3 Open the telephone book to a center page. Place the first valley fold of the concertina (the fold between the "cover" and the first mountain fold) into the gulley of the phone book. Place the first signature, opened to its center page, into this valley fold, and then lay the pattern on top. Press the concertina, signature, and pattern down into the gully of the phone book.

4 Use the awl to punch holes in the fold, following the pattern. When you finish, carefully remove the signature (but not the concertina) and set it aside, being sure to keep it oriented as it was while you punched the holes.

5 Move the concertina so that the second valley fold is in the gully of the phone book. Press the next signature into the gully on top of the concertina. Lay the pattern on top and repeat step 4. Continue until you have punched all the signatures and valley folds.

SEWING THE FIRST SIGNATURE/ CONCERTINA TO THE COVER

6 After you've punched all the holes, thread the needle with 2 yards (1.8 m) of thread. Pick up the first signature, insert it into the first concertina fold, and place it inside the front cover. Insert the needle from the outside into the first hole from the bottom. Be sure to pull the thread parallel to the paper's surface and not straight up to avoid tearing. Pull the thread through, leaving a 5-inch (12.7 cm) tail. Clip the tail to the cover with a paper clip to keep it from pulling through before you tie it off.

7 Put the needle into the second hole, from the inside to the outside. Pull the thread through and over the first strap in the cover's spine. Then insert the needle into the next hole, back to the inside of the signature.

8 Repeat step 7 to sew over all the remaining straps until you reach the last strap at the top or head of the cover. Bring the needle out the last hole of the signature from the inside, and then pause.

ADDING MORE SIGNATURES WITH CONCERTINA FOLDS

9 Pick up the second signature and place it into the second concertina fold. Lay it snuggly next to the first, already-sewn signature. Put the needle, from the outside, into the top hole of the second signature (just across from the top hole of the first signature).

10 Pull the thread through, and put the needle into the second hole, from the inside. Pull the needle over the top strap and then into the next hole down (just past the strap), back to the inside of the signature.

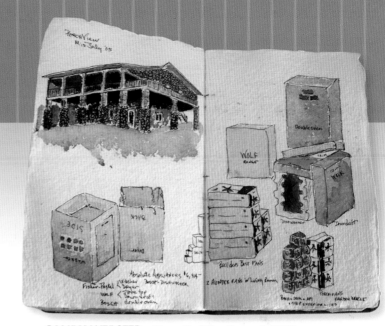

SANDY WEBSTER *House Building Journal,* **2005**
8 x 6 x 2 inches (20.3 x 15.2 x 5.1 cm); watercolors, pen PHOTO BY ARTIST

11 Continue sewing over all the straps to the bottom of the second signature. When you come out of the last hole, just across from the hole at the bottom of the first signature with the tail hanging out, carefully tie the tail to the thread to secure the first two signatures. Do not cut the thread, but continue sewing by putting the needle into the bottom hole of the third signature and concertina fold.

12 Repeat steps 7 and 8. Before you put the needle into the first hole of each new signature, scoop between the last two signatures, as in figure 2. The scoop stitch ties the signatures together. After scooping, put the needle into the first hole of the new signature and continue sewing.

13 When you get to the end of the last signature/ concertina fold, tie off the thread on the outside of the signature (see Bookbinding Essentials). If you want a cleaner look to the spine, dab a little PVA on the cut ends of the knots at the first and last signatures. Then tuck the thread ends up under the cover straps.

Coptic Binding

This basic Coptic binding, which works with both hard and soft covers, allows the book to open and stay flat. Its open spine makes for a flexible book, to which you can add flat elements such as collage, extra pages, and photographs (in moderation) without causing the front or foredge to splay open. You can tighten or fatten the spine by adding a concertina (page 92). A Coptic binding also lends itself to double books (page 101). If you want a tighter binding, and if the desired cover boards are at least ⅛ inch (3 mm) thick, try the Three-Hole Coptic binding (page 104).

WHAT YOU NEED

Bookbinding Tool Kit (page 47)

2 hard or soft cover boards (page 142) for a simple Coptic binding or 3 boards for a double book, such as the book on page 31)

Scrap paper, 2 inches (5.1 cm) x the height of the text pages

Text pages in signatures (see Bookbinding Essentials)

Curved needle

3-ply bookbinder's thread, 3–5 yards (2.7–4.6 m) depending on the book size (see Note)

Note: In this binding style, the thread is a design element since you can see it on the outside of the spine, so choose the color with design in mind.

GWEN DIEHN **Untitled, 2009**
4 x 6 x ¾ inches (10.2 x 15.2 x 1.9 cm);
Coptic binding with hard cover

WHAT YOU DO

PREPARING THE COVERS

1 Hold the two cover boards together, oriented as they'll be in the finished book. Pencil mark on the top cover where you want the sewing stations or holes, which should be at least ½ inch (1.3 cm) in from any edge to avoid tearing. Figure 1 shows a couple of sample patterns.

2 Lay the covers, still together, on the telephone book (to protect the tabletop). Poke the holes you've marked in both covers at the same time. Twist the awl in a screw-like motion while pressing down. You may not be able to poke the bottom cover holes all the way through; that's fine as long as you at least mark them. Remove the top cover and finish poking the holes in the bottom one.

MAKING THE SIGNATURES

3 Fold the piece of scrap paper in half lengthwise. Align it with the row of holes in one of the covers so that it's centered the way the text pages will be. Pencil mark the position of the holes in the fold of the scrap paper pattern (figure 2).

4 Cut or tear the text pages to size, and fold each one individually to form folios. Depending on the thickness of the paper, nest between two and six folios into one another to form signatures (see Bookbinding Essentials).

5 Place each signature in turn, with its pages carefully lined up, in the fold of the telephone book, pressing its center fold down into the gully, as shown in Bookbinding Essentials. Lay the pattern over the center of the signature, pressing the fold of the pattern down into the center gully. Use the awl to punch holes in the signature. When you finish each signature, remove it,

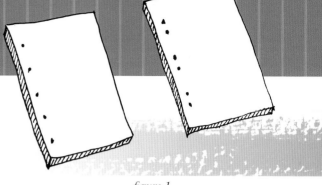

figure 1

figure 2

SARAH BOURNE *Daily Journal*, 2005
8½ x 11 inches (21.6 x 27.9 cm); hand-bound journal; watercolors, pencil, collage PHOTO BY ARTIST

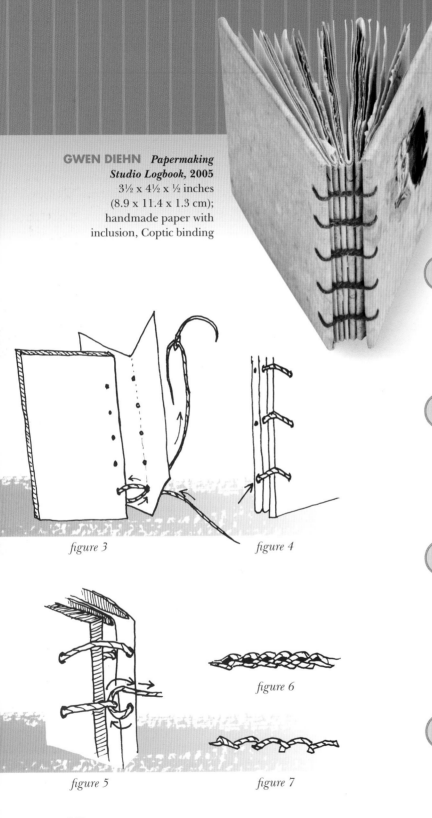

figure 3

figure 4

figure 5

figure 6

figure 7

keeping the top of the pages facing up. Repeat this step until you've punched holes in every signature.

SEWING THE FIRST SIGNATURE TO THE COVER

6 Thread the curved needle with about 2 yards (1.8 m) of thread, and tie a knot in one end of the thread. Pick up one cover (it doesn't matter which) and the signature you want next to it. Open the signature and insert the needle into either the top or bottom hole from the inside. Pull the thread through until the knot rests against the hole.

7 Reach around the cover, and insert the needle into the corresponding hole of the cover from the outside. Pull the thread through between the cover and the first signature, pulling in the direction of the spine and not straight up. Poke the needle back into the first hole of the signature from the outside (figure 3).

CONNECTING THE SECOND SIGNATURE

8 Move the needle and thread up to the next hole inside the signature and repeat step 7 until you've sewn through all but one of the cover holes. When you get to the last cover hole, sew through it, joining the cover to the first signature, but then stop. Do not insert the needle and thread back into the last hole of the first signature. Instead, pick up the second signature and enter the needle into its first hole from the outside (figure 4).

9 Now the needle is inside the next signature. Insert it into the second hole, from the inside, and pull the thread through. On the outside, use the curve of the needle to scoop the little piece of thread that's between the cover and the first signature. Scoop toward the top of the book if you are sewing toward the bottom (figure 5) in order to keep the stitches uniform. Then put the needle back through the same hole of the second signature from the outside. Repeat this step until you've sewn all holes in the second signature.

COMPLETING THE BOOK

10 Repeat step 9 to connect and sew up the rest of the signatures. Once you have sewn the second signature, however, *always scoop the thread between the signature you are sewing and the one you just finished*. Do not go back and scoop the thread between the cover and the first signature once you have finished with that signature, or the spine will curl in tightly. The scoop stitches should form a chain stitch on the outside of the spine (figure 6). The top and bottom rows look a little different because you make only half chains in those rows (figure 7).

11 Attach the second cover as you did the first. You'll already have sewn a row of stitches inside the last signature, but this isn't a problem. Simply lay the new thread on top of the thread that's already there. After the last stitch, which puts the needle inside the signature, tie off and trim the thread (see Bookbinding Essentials).

MAKING A DOUBLE COPTIC BOOK

12 If you want to make a double Coptic book, choose either a gatefold (figure 8) or a dos-à-dos (figure 9).

13 Make three cover boards, as in figure 10 (for a gatefold) or figure 11 (for a dos-à-dos). Follow directions for the kind of covers you want (page 142). Sew the books exactly the same as for any other Coptic, but make a row of stitches on both sides of the shared cover.

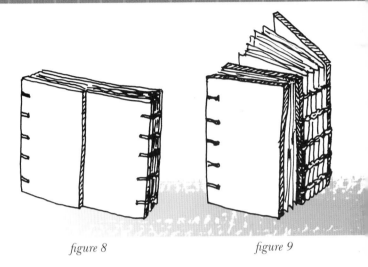

figure 8   figure 9

figure 10

figure 11

Coptic with Concertina

A basic Coptic binding (page 98) has an uncovered spine, meaning the folds of the signatures are exposed. Adding a concertina to a Coptic binding closes the spine somewhat, as the concertina folds protect the text pages. You can also use the concertina folds themselves as slipcases, envelopes, or stubs for adding other elements. The directions for a Coptic binding with a concertina are the same as for a basic Coptic except that you nest each signature in a fold of the concertina and whatever you do to the signature (such as punching holes and sewing), you do to the concertina at the same time.

FRAN LOGES *New Learning Journal*, **2009**
5 x 8½ inches (12.7 x 21.6 cm); magazine page bound into
the book using a concertina fold and a paper pin to anchor it

WHAT YOU NEED

Bookbinding Tool Kit (page 47)

*Text pages in signatures
(see Bookbinding Essentials)*

*2 hard or soft cover boards (see page 142)
or 3 boards for a double book, such as the
book on page 31)*

Concertina paper (see step 1)

*Scrap paper, 2 inches (5.1 cm) x the height
of the text pages*

*3-ply bookbinder's thread, 3–5 yards
(2.7–4.6 m) or more, depending on the
book size (see Note)*

Curved needle

Note: If in doubt, get more thread. In this binding style, you can see the thread on the outside of the spine, so choose the color with design in mind.

JAN WHEATCROFT *Sri Lanka; Ulpotha,* **2000**
7 x 5 inches (17.8 x 12.7 cm); pen, watercolors
PHOTO BY GENARO MOLINA

WHAT YOU DO

1 Construct a concertina (page 92). Based on the paper thickness of the individual folios, nest two to five folios into one another to form signatures (see Bookbinding Essentials).

2 Turn to the basic Coptic directions (page 98) and follow steps 1 through 4 to prepare the covers and the signatures. Then return to this page and continue with the steps below.

3 Open the telephone book to a center page. Follow the directions to make a pattern and punch out sewing stations as described in the Bookbinding Essentials with the following modification: Place the first valley fold of the concertina (the fold between the cover and the first mountain fold) into the gulley of the phone book. Place the first signature into this valley fold, and then lay the pattern on top. Press the concertina, signature, and pattern down into the gully of the phone book.

4 Use the awl to punch holes in the fold, following the pattern. When you finish, carefully remove the signature (but not the concertina) and set it aside, being sure to keep it oriented as it was while you punched the holes.

5 Move the concertina so that the second valley fold is in the gully of the phone book. Press the next signature into the gully on top of the concertina. Lay the pattern on top and repeat step 4. Continue until you have punched all the signatures and valley folds.

6 Return to the basic Coptic directions (page 100) and follow steps 6 through 11 to sew the signatures and the covers together. Remember: When you sew the book, sew the concertina and signature together as one unit.

Three-Hole Coptic

The Three-Hole Coptic is a nice variation of the Coptic stitch that results in a book with a tighter spine. If you're making a hardcover Coptic book with a cover board that's at least ⅛ inch (3 mm) thick, you might want to try it. The cover is more closely attached to the text block, so there is less space between the individual signatures.

WHAT YOU NEED

Bookbinding Tool Kit (page 47)

2 Davey boards

Scrap paper, 2 inches (5.1 cm) x the height of the text pages

Text pages in signatures (see Bookbinding Essentials)

Curved needle

Straight needle (optional, see Note)

3-ply bookbinder's thread, 3–5 yards (2.7–4.6 m) depending on the book size (see Note)

GWEN DIEHN   Untitled, 2009
5 x 7 x 1 inches (12.7 x 17.8 x 2.5 cm); Three-Hole Coptic binding with a paper-covered hard cover

Note: In this binding style, the thread is a design element since you can see it on the outside of the spine, so choose the color with design in mind. It also helps to use a thin awl because of the holes you have to make in the ends of the boards. You might also want to have a straight needle on hand in case you have problems getting a curved needle through some of the holes.

WHAT YOU DO

1 Hold the two cover boards together, oriented as they'll be in the finished book. Open the telephone book to a middle page and lay the two covers down on one side. Pencil mark the sewing stations: one about ¼ inch (6 mm) in from the edge (which is closer to the edge than usual, but because you'll make two holes at the top of the book, the main stress is on the one that's farther in), a second about ½ inch (1.3 cm) in from the edge, and a third actually *in* the edge—it's a branching tunnel (figure 1).

2 Use the awl to poke the two surface holes at each station. Do both covers at the same time. Twist the awl in a screw-like motion while pressing down. You may not be able to poke the bottom cover holes all the way through; that's fine as long as you at least mark them. Remove the top cover and finish poking the holes in the bottom one.

3 To punch the edge holes, pick up the covers one at a time and push the thin awl into the edge at the mark. As you push, angle the direction slightly so that the tip of the awl comes out the closest surface hole on the top surface of the board (figure 2).

4 Then push the awl into the same edge hole, but this time angle the hole slightly downward so that the tip pokes out of the closest edge hole on the bottom surface of the cover (figure 3). Repeat for all edge holes on both covers.

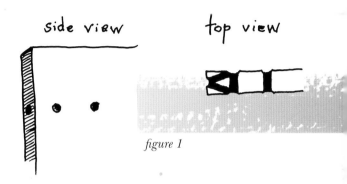

figure 1

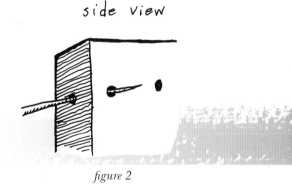

figure 2

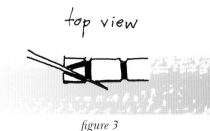

figure 3

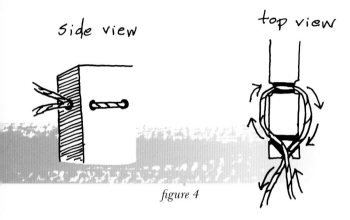

side view   top view

figure 4

figure 5

figure 6

5 When you've poked all the holes you need in the covers, refer to the basic Coptic instructions (page 98) and follow steps 3 to 6.

6 After you've pulled the needle and thread out of the first hole of the signature, insert the needle into the first edge hole of a cover board, aiming the needle either up or down (toward one of the surface holes). Pull the thread gently out of the surface hole until the stitch is snug. Then insert the needle into the farther-out surface hole, pulling the thread through. At this point, you've sewn in through the edge and through both surface holes. All you need to do now is sew back into the surface hole closest to the edge and aim the needle toward the edge, using the tunnel you haven't used yet. In other words, if you slanted down when you first entered the edge hole, slant up to exit (figure 4).

7 When you exit the edge hole, pull everything snug, and then re-enter the first hole of the signature to put the needle back to the inside (figure 5).

8 Move to the next sewing station/hole, and exit the signature as in figure 6. Sew each station the same way until you finish the last one. Stop before inserting the needle back into the signature. Instead, pick up the second signature and enter the needle into its first hole from the outside.

9 Follow steps 9, 10, and 11 of the basic Coptic instructions (page 100) to attach the rest of the signatures and the back cover.

Sewn on Tapes

The Sewn on Tapes binding is strong enough to hold books with many pages. Choose from several kinds of covers, depending on what best fits your purpose. You can glue the sewn text block into a hard cover (page 147) or into an unmounted piece of leather or canvas (page 133). Another option is to lace it into a heavy paper cover (page 136) or into a leather cover (page 139).

WHAT YOU NEED

Bookbinding Tool Kit (page 47)

Text pages in folios (see Bookbinding Essentials)

Scrap paper for the pattern, 2 inches (5.1 cm) x the height of the text pages

3 pieces of ½-inch (1.3 cm) wide ribbon or bookbinder's cloth tape, as long as the spine's width plus 4 to 6 inches (10.2 to 15.2 cm)

2-ply bookbinder's thread

Straight needle

Thin paper, the spine's width x the spine's length minus ¼ inch (6 mm)

Strong paper, the spine's length x 4 inches (10.2 cm)

Optional headband (page 52)

2 pieces of plain or decorative end paper, the same size as the text pages

Chosen cover

JUDITH GOLDEN *Florence Journal,* **2000**
12 x 8¼ x ¾ inches (30.5 x 21 x 1.9 cm); various papers, collage, ribbon, green & gold ink, western codex Sewn on Tapes PHOTO BY PAT BARRETT

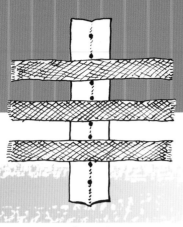

figure 1

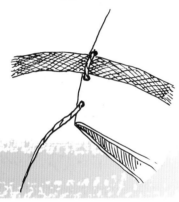

figure 2

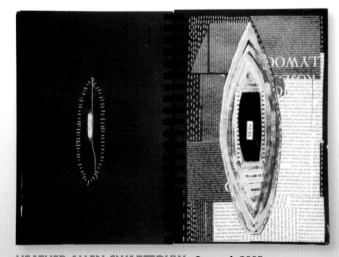

HEATHER ALLEN-SWARTTOUW Journal, 2005
6 x 8 inches (15.2 x 20.3 cm); hand-bound journal,
stitching; collage, white gouache on black paper

WHAT YOU DO

PREPARING THE SIGNATURES

1 Assemble the signatures of text pages folded in folios (see Bookbinding Essentials). Avoid overstuffed signatures. It's best to use at least five signatures, even if each has only a few pages.

2 Before punching holes for sewing, you need to make a pattern. Fold the 2-inch-wide (5.1 cm) strip of scrap paper in half lengthwise. Crease the center fold, and then unfold it. Fold it in half again, this time in the other direction. Crease and unfold again. The creased cross marks the exact center of the paper. Lay a piece of binder's tape across the center point.

3 Make a pencil mark in the lengthwise crease above and below the tape. Measure ½ inch (1.3 cm) up from the bottom of the paper and mark in the crease again. Repeat ½ inch (1.3 cm) down from the top. Place the second binder's tape at a point midway between the middle and bottom marks. Make pencil marks in the crease above and below the tape. Repeat between the middle and top marks with the third binder's tape. You will make eight holes in all (figure 1).

4 Follow the directions for punching holes using a telephone directory in Bookbinding Essentials. Punch all the pattern marks into each signature.

SEWING THE SIGNATURES TOGETHER

5 Thread the needle with a single strand of thread about 2 yards (1.8 m) long. Do not tie a knot in the thread. Pick up the first signature and stick the needle through the bottom hole from the outside. Leave a 5-inch (12.7 cm) tail hanging out.

6 Place the first piece of binder's tape between the next two holes on the outside of the signature. From inside the signature, bring the needle out of the next hole, run it over the tape, and insert it back to the inside in the hole on the other side of the tape (figure 2). Place the second piece of tape between the two center holes. Sew out of the signature through the next hole and pull the thread over the second tape. Insert the needle back to the inside through the hole on the other side of the tape. Repeat this step for the third piece of tape.

7 At the top of the signature, pick up the second signature and insert the needle into the top hole from the outside. Repeat step 6 for the second signature (although the tape is already in place across the back of the spine).

8 When you're ready for the third signature, make sure all your stitches are tight. (See Bookbinding Essentials for sewing tips.) Before sewing into the new signature, tie the tail to the thread on the needle (figure 3). Then continue sewing the third signature as you did the other two, starting at the bottom hole.

9 Before sewing into the fourth signature, scoop the little stitch between the second and third signatures to link them to the new signature (figure 4). Repeat this scoop stitch before attaching each new signature to the book. It links the signatures together at both top and bottom.

10 After you've sewn all the folds, scoop the last stitch and return the needle to the inside to tie it off, using the knot described in Bookbinding Essentials. Cut all the thread ends to ½ inch (1.3 cm) and tug gently at the tapes so they lie evenly across the signatures.

Note: If you're going to *lace* the straps into a flexible cover (page 136), skip ahead to step 18. If you're going to *glue* the book to a cover, continue with step 11.

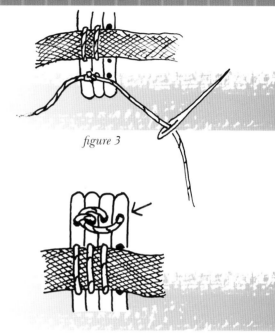

figure 3

figure 4

KONRAD ZOLL
The Chatter Box Grill, **2005**
10 x 5 inches (25.4 x 12.7 cm);
graphite on paper
PHOTO BY ARTIST

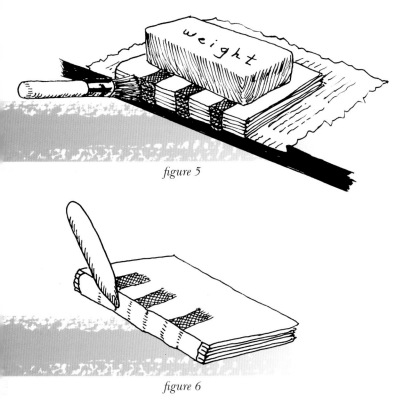

figure 5

figure 6

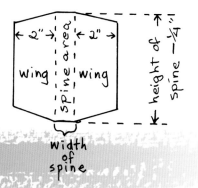

figure 7

BACKING THE SPINE

11 The next few steps make the spine stronger and ready to glue to the cover. Tear out a few pages from the telephone book and lay them on the edge of a table. Place the text block on top of them, pressing it down gently with your hand. With your other hand, gently pound some PVA into the spine with the brush (figure 5). The object is to push a little PVA into the spaces between the signatures so that they stick together enough to conceal the backing. Gently compress the text block as you pound so you don't push the PVA too deeply into the pages, which will make the book hard to open. Cover the spine's surface completely, including the tapes where they cross. PVA remains flexible when it dries, providing strength to the spine while allowing you to easily open and turn the pages.

12 While the spine dries, brush PVA over one side of the piece of thin paper (which will become the spine stiffener). Center it over the spine, glue side down, and press it in place. With the bone folder or your hands (my preference), burnish the stiffener into the bumps and ridges of the spine (figure 6).

ATTACHING THE TEXT BLOCK TO THE COVER

13 The next step is to make a hinge, which will help fasten the text block to the cover. Using the piece of strong paper, follow the diagrams for measuring and cutting a hinge in figure 7.

14 Brush PVA onto only the spine strip in the center of the hinge. Then press and burnish the hinge to the spine (figure 8). Do not glue the wings of the hinge to the text block; you'll attach them to the inside of the cover later.

15 To add headbands (an optional step), follow the directions on page 52, using PVA to glue one to the spine's head and one to the tail, right on top of the hinge ends (figure 9). Clean up any excess glue and let everything dry completely.

16 Next, tip in the two end papers. Fold both into folios so that the decorated sides (if applicable) are on the inside. Lay a piece of scrap paper with at least one straight side ¼ inch (6 mm) in from the fold on one side of the first folio. Brush PVA carefully along the exposed strip (figure 10).

17 Line up the gluey strip against the spine edge of the text block, tucking it carefully under the hinge and the loose ends of the sewing tapes. Burnish it firmly with a bone folder to adhere it to the first page of the text block (figure 11). Repeat for the end paper folio on the other side of the book. Let everything dry completely before proceeding.

18 The final step is to attach the text block to its cover. Follow the directions on one of the following pages, depending on your selected cover. You can glue the text block into a hard cover (page 147) or a flexible leather or heavy cloth cover (page 133). You can also lace it into a heavy paper or leather cover (page 136).

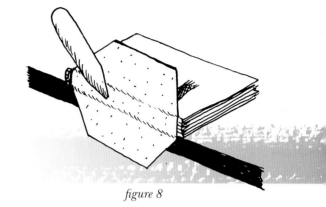

figure 8

figure 9   *figure 10*

figure 11

Sewn on Tapes with Concertina

n this version of the Sewn on Tapes binding, a concertina provides protection for text pages, as well as pleats for different kinds of flat elements. Deeper pleats can become double-layer pages, slipcases, or envelopes. The Sewn on Tapes binding is very strong and works well with several kinds of covers.

WHAT YOU NEED

Bookbinding Tool Kit (page 47)

Text pages in folios (see Bookbinding Essentials)

Concertina (page 92)

Scrap paper for the pattern, 2 inches (5.1 cm) x the height of the text pages

3 pieces of ½-inch (1.3 cm) wide ribbon or bookbinder's cloth tape, as long as the spine's width plus 4 to 6 inches (10.2 to 15.2 cm)— plus 8 inches (20.3 cm) for a flexible cover with a laced-in text block

2-ply bookbinder's thread

Straight needle

Thin paper, the spine's width x the spine's length minus ¼ inch (6 mm)

Strong paper, the spine's length x 5 inches (12.7 cm)

Optional headband (page 52)

Chosen cover into which to glue or lace the text block (page 133, 136, or 147)

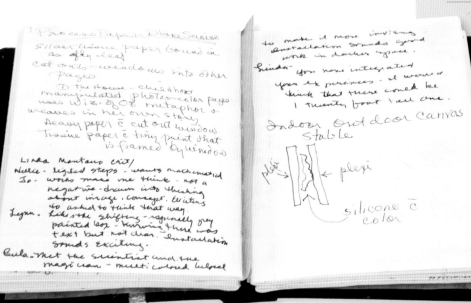

GWEN DIEHN   **Untitled, 1998**
6 x 8 x ½ inches (15.2 x 20.3 x 1.3 cm);
Sewn on Tapes with concertina book

WHAT YOU DO

PREPARING THE SIGNATURES AND CONCERTINA

1 Assemble the folios of text pages into signatures, and slip one signature into each pleat of the concertina (figure 1). It's best to use at least five signatures, even if each has only a few pages in it. Avoid overstuffing the signatures.

2 Before punching holes for sewing, you need to make a pattern. Fold the 2-inch-wide (5.1 cm) strip of scrap paper in half lengthwise. Crease the center fold, and then unfold it. Fold it in half again in the other direction. Crease and unfold it. The place where the creases cross is the center of the pattern. Lay a piece of binder's tape across the center point (figure 2).

3 Make a pencil mark in the lengthwise crease above and below the tape. Measure ½ inch (1.3 cm) up from the bottom of the paper and mark in the crease again. Repeat ½ inch (1.3 cm) down from the top. Place the second binder's tape at a point midway between the middle and bottom marks. Make pencil marks in the crease above and below the tape. Repeat between the middle and top marks with the third binder's tape. You will make eight holes in all (figure 3).

4 Open the telephone directory to a middle page. Remove all signatures from the concertina except the first one—but keep them handy and in order. Lay the first concertina pleat and its signature in the gutter of the phone book, and then place the pattern on top of it (see Bookbinding Essentials for details). *Note: From this point forward, treat the signature and its concertina pleat as a single unit.* Press the signature and the pattern into the gutter. Punch holes at every mark on the pattern into the signature. Carefully remove the signature from the phone book and lay the pattern aside.

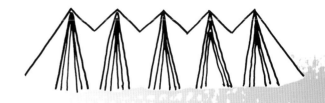

figure 1

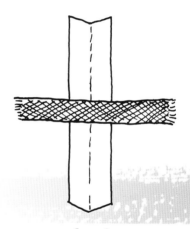

figure 2

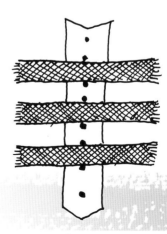

figure 3

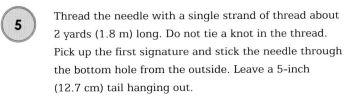

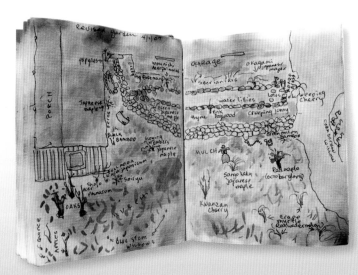

figure 4

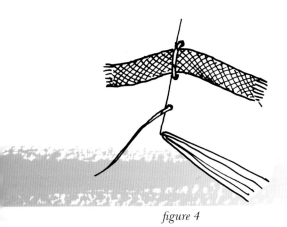

SANDY WEBSTER *House Building Journal,* **2005**
8 x 6 x 2 inches (20.3 x 15.2 x 5.1 cm); pen,
watercolors made from local clay PHOTO BY ARTIST

SEWING THE SIGNATURES AND CONCERTINA TOGETHER

5 Thread the needle with a single strand of thread about 2 yards (1.8 m) long. Do not tie a knot in the thread. Pick up the first signature and stick the needle through the bottom hole from the outside. Leave a 5-inch (12.7 cm) tail hanging out.

6 Place the first piece of binder's tape between the next two holes on the outside of the signature. Bring the needle out of the next hole, run it over the tape, and insert it back to the inside in the hole on the other side of the tape (figure 4). Place the second piece of tape between the two center holes. Sew out of the signature through the next hole and pull the thread over the second tape. Insert the needle back to the inside through the hole on the other side of the tape. Repeat this process for the third piece of tape.

7 When you reach the top of the signature, put aside the needle and thread without cutting the thread. Lay the second signature in its concertina pleat in the gutter of the phone book and place the pattern on top. Press both the signature and pattern into the gutter. Punch holes from the pattern into the signature. Carefully remove the signature from the phone book and lay the pattern aside. Pick up the second signature and place the threaded needle into the first hole at the top of the second signature. Repeat step 6 for the second signature (although the tape is already in place across the back of the spine).

8 When you're ready to sew the third signature, make sure all stitches are tight. (See Bookbinding Essentials for sewing tips.) Before you sew into the bottom hole of the new signature, tie the hanging tail to the thread on the needle. Then continue sewing the third signature as you did the other two.

9 Before sewing into the fourth signature, scoop the little stitch between the second and third signatures to link them together (figure 5). Repeat this scoop stitch before you add each new signature to the book. It links the signatures together at both top and bottom, holding the book together.

10 After you've sewn all the signatures, scoop the last stitch and return the needle to the inside to tie it off, using the knot described in Bookbinding Essentials. Cut all the thread ends to ½ inch (1.3 cm) and tug gently at the tapes so they lie evenly across the signatures.

Note: If you're going to *lace* the straps into a flexible cover (page 136), skip ahead to step 16. If you're going to *glue* the book to a cover, continue with step 11.

BACKING THE SPINE

11 The next few steps make the spine stronger and ready to glue to the cover. Tear out a few pages from the telephone book and lay them on the edge of a table. Place the text block on top of them, pressing it down gently with your hand. With your other hand, gently pound some PVA into the spine with the brush (figure 6). The object is to pound a little PVA into the spaces between the signatures so that they stick together enough to conceal the backing. Gently compress the text block as you pound so you don't push the PVA too deeply into the pages. Cover the spine's surface completely, including the tapes where they cross. PVA remains flexible when it dries, providing strength to the spine while allowing you to easily turn the pages.

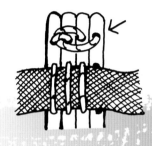

figure 5

figure 6

figure 7

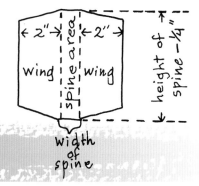

figure 8

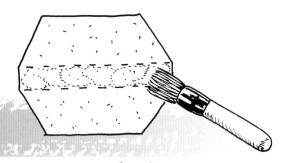

figure 9

12 While the spine dries, brush PVA over one side of the piece of thin paper (which will become the spine stiffener). Center it over the spine, glue side down, and press it in place. With the bone folder or your hands (my preference), burnish the stiffener into the bumps and ridges of the spine (figure 7).

ATTACHING THE TEXT BLOCK TO THE COVER

13 The next step is to make a hinge, which will help fasten the text block to the cover. Using the strong paper, follow the diagrams for measuring and cutting a hinge in figure 8.

14 Brush PVA onto only the spine strip in the center of the hinge (figure 9). Then press and burnish the hinge to the spine. Do not glue the wings of the hinge to the text block; you'll attach them to the inside of the cover later.

15 To add headbands (an optional step), follow the directions on page 52, using PVA to glue one to the spine's head and one to the tail, right on top of the hinge ends (figure 9 again). Clean up any excess glue and let everything dry completely.

16 The final step is to attach the text block to the cover. The large front and back pages of the concertina itself can serve as end pages if you glue the book into a hard or flexible cover. To glue the text block into a hard cover, see page 147. To glue it into a flexible leather or heavy cloth cover, see page 133. To lace it into a heavy paper or leather cover, see page 136.

Accordion
Sewn on Tapes

The text pages of this book are held together in part by cloth bookbinder's tapes that span the spine. Because the text block is made of an accordion, the book's pages are doubled, folded on the foredge. Double pages are ideal for painting, printing, drawing, and even heavy collage because they won't allow bleed-through. You can make some or all of the double pages into pockets by gluing or stitching across the bottom.

WHAT YOU NEED

Bookbinding Tool Kit (page 47)

Text pages folded in reverse folios (see step 1)

Scrap paper for the pattern, 2 inches (5.1 cm) x the height of the text pages

3 lengths of ½-inch-wide (1.3 cm) bookbinder's cloth tape (or ribbon), each 6 inches (15.2 cm) long plus the width of the book's spine

2-ply bookbinder's thread

Straight needle

Thin paper for the spine stiffener, spine height x spine width

Strong paper for the hinge, 4 inches (10.2 cm) plus the spine width x the spine height

Headband (optional)

2 pieces of end paper

Cover of your choice

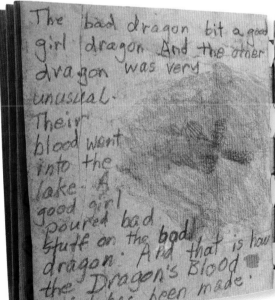

MAYA DIEHN AND GWEN DIEHN *Outings Journal, 2007–2009*
5 x 5 x 1 inches (12.7 x 12.7 x 2.5 cm); Accordion Sewn on Tapes book made of a grocery bag sewn over straps made from the bag handle; pen, crayons, watercolors, gouache

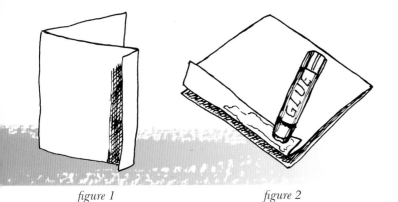

figure 1

figure 2

figure 3

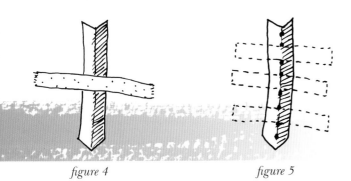

figure 4

figure 5

WHAT YOU DO

ASSEMBLING THE ACCORDION

1 Fold each text page with an extra inch on one side (figure 1). This strip becomes the glue tab to connect the pages into an accordion. Apply the glue stick to the outside of the first tab (figure 2).

2 Lay the next folio, glue tab up, on top of the first one and press down on the left edge (figure 3) to set the glue. Repeat for all folios to make a long, deep-pleated accordion.

PREPARING AND USING THE PATTERN

3 Before punching holes for sewing, you need to make a pattern. Fold the 2-inch-wide (5.1 cm) strip of scrap paper in half lengthwise. Crease the center fold, and then unfold it. Fold it in half again, this time in the other direction. Crease and unfold again. The creased cross marks the exact center of the paper. Lay a piece of binder's tape across the center point (figure 4).

4 Make a pencil mark in the lengthwise crease above and below the tape. Measure ½ inch (1.3 cm) up from the bottom of the paper and mark in the crease again. Repeat ½ inch (1.3 cm) down from the top. Move the binder's tape to a point midway between the middle and bottom marks. Make pencil marks in the crease above and below the tape. Repeat between the middle and top marks (figure 5).

5 Open the telephone book to a middle page, as shown in Bookbinding Essentials. Lay the first fold of the accordion (between the first two pages) in the gutter of the page, and place the pattern on top of it. Press both the fold and the pattern into the gutter. Use the awl to punch holes in the spine folds of the accordion.

SEWING THE ACCORDION FOLDS TOGETHER

6 This first fold is the hardest to hold and sew. Thread the needle with about 2 yards (1.8 m) of thread. Pick up the first fold of the accordion and enter it through the bottom hole from the outside, leaving a 5-inch (12.7 cm) tail hanging out. Bring the needle out though the next hole. Place a piece of binder's tape between this hole and the next one on the outside of the fold. Pull the thread over the tape, and then put the needle into the hole on the other side of the tape (figure 6). If the accordion threatens to leap out of your hands, rest the folds on the table in a pile. As you sew, you'll get better at this. Take deep breaths!

7 Place the second piece of tape between the two center holes. Bring the needle out the next hole and pull it over the second tape. Repeat for the third piece of tape and the next set of holes. At the top of the fold, exit the last hole, pick up the second fold, and insert the needle into the top hole. Repeat these steps, sewing in and out of the fold to secure the binder's tape (figure 6 again).

8 When you're ready for the third fold, make sure all your stitches are tight. (Check Bookbinding Essentials for sewing tips.) Then tie the tail to the thread that's on the needle. Continue sewing the third fold as you did the others, starting at the bottom hole (figure 6 again). Before putting the needle into the first (top) hole of the fourth fold, scoop the little stitch between the two previous folds to link them together (figure 7). Repeat this scoop stitch before attaching each new fold. This scoop stitch is essential, as it links the folds together at the top and bottom.

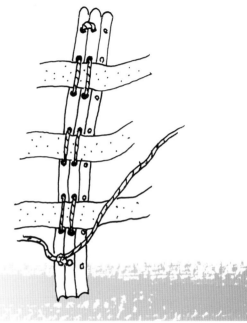

figure 6

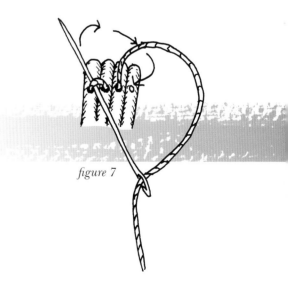

figure 7

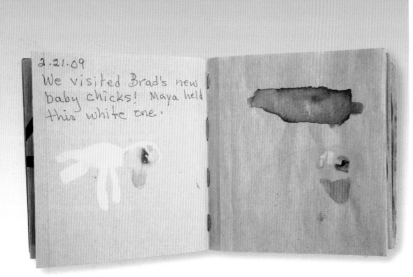

MAYA DIEHN AND GWEN DIEHN *Outings Journal,* 2007–2009
5 x 5 x 1 inches (12.7 x 12.7 x 2.5 cm); Accordion Sewn on Tapes
binding made of a grocery bag sewn over straps made from the bag
handle with a self cover; pen, crayon, watercolors, gouache

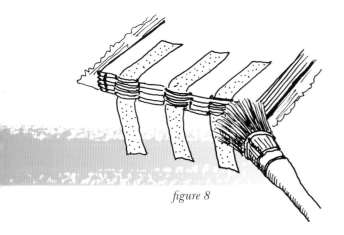

figure 8

9 After you've sewn all the folds, scoop the last stitch and return the needle to the inside to tie it off, using the knot described in Bookbinding Essentials. Cut all the thread ends to ½ inch (1.3 cm) and tug gently at the tapes to make them lie evenly across the signatures.

Note: If you're going to *lace* the straps into a flexible cover (page 136), skip ahead to step 14. If you're going to *glue* the book to a cover, continue with step 10.

BACKING THE SPINE

10 The next few steps make the spine stronger and ready to glue to the cover. Tear out a few pages from the telephone book and lay them on the edge of a table. Place the text block on top of them, pressing it down gently with your hand. With your other hand, gently pound PVA into the spine with the brush (figure 8). The goal is to get the PVA a short distance into the spaces between the folds so that the folds stick together enough to conceal the backing. Gently compress the text block as you pound so you don't push the PVA too deeply into the pages, thereby making the book hard to open. Cover the spine's surface completely, including the tapes where they cross. PVA remains flexible when it dries, providing strength to the spine while allowing you to easily open and turn the pages.

11 While the spine dries, cut a piece of thin paper the width of the spine by ¼ inch (6 mm) shorter than the height to use as a spine stiffener. Brush PVA over one side of the stiffener, center it over the spine, and press it in place. Burnish the spine stiffener into the bumps and ridges of the spine with a bone folder or—my preference—your finger (figure 9). The text block is now ready for you to attach to the cover.

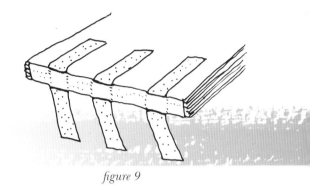

figure 9

ATTACHING THE TEXT BLOCK TO THE COVER

12 We'll use a hinge to help fasten the text block to the cover. Using the piece of strong paper, follow the diagrams for measuring and cutting a hinge in figure 10. Brush PVA onto only the spine strip in the center of the hinge. Then press and burnish the hinge to the spine. Do not glue the wings of the hinge to the text block; you'll attach them to the inside of the cover later, which the end papers will hide (figure 11).

13 To add headbands (an optional step), follow the directions on page 52, using PVA to glue one to the spine's head and one to the tail, right on top of the hinge ends. Clean up any excess glue and let everything dry completely.

14 You can glue this text block into a hard cover (page 147) or a flexible leather or heavy cloth cover (page 133). You can also lace it into a heavy paper or leather cover (page 136) or use a self cover.

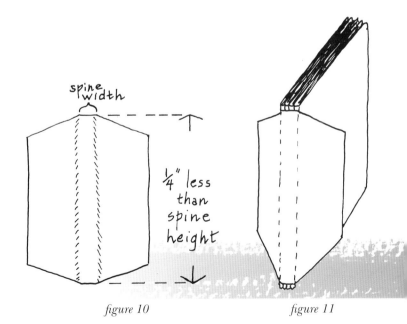

figure 10 *figure 11*

CHAPTER 5

10 cover instructions

Each set of book form instructions in Chapter Four lists which general kinds of covers (flexible or hard-cover or even self cover or double cover) are appropriate for that binding style. Once you find out which general types will work, browse through the cover instructions in Chapter Five to determine which will best do the job you need it to do. For example, if you're going to make a Coptic binding, you'll learn that there are several kinds of covers that will work for that binding— metal, folded paper, hard cover, etc. Check out each option and choose the one that best fits your purpose. Then follow the instructions to make your cover.

Australian Reversed Piano Hinge Self Cover

This is the easiest self cover around. Use it as a model for other self covers, especially for simple Pamphlet books. This cover works for the round style as well as the flat style of Australian Reversed Piano Hinge bindings, and also for any binding that involves a concertina. Try it with small, informal Sewn on Tapes books, too.

WHAT YOU NEED

Bookbinding Tool Kit (page 47)

Scrap paper, such as an old telephone directory

2 rags: 1 damp and 1 dry

GWEN DIEHN *Boat Journal,* 2008
4 x 6½ x ½ inches (10.2 x 16.5 x 1.3 cm); Round-Style Australian Reversed Piano Hinge with self cover; poured acrylic, watercolor, pen

figure 1

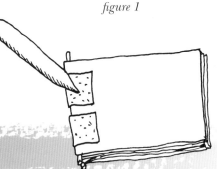

figure 2

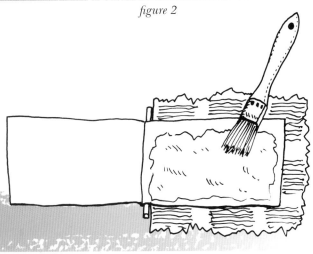

figure 3

WHAT YOU DO

1 Find the little pleat(s) or leftover piece(s) of concertina or binding tape on the cover of the text block. Open them out over the scrap paper, and brush PVA all over the surface that faces you (figure 1).

2 Remove the scrap paper, wipe off your hands, and press the gluey surface to the first text page, as in figure 2. Turn the book over and repeat steps 1 and 2.

3 Fold open the first text page—which has the little leftover concertina piece(s) already glued to it—and put a piece of scrap paper under the next text page (figure 3). Brush PVA all over it.

4 Remove the scrap paper, wipe off your hands, and press the gluey surface to the next text page. You have laminated two pages together, and when the PVA dries, the resulting page becomes a heavier, more durable cover. Repeat steps 3 and 4 for the other side of the book to make the back cover.

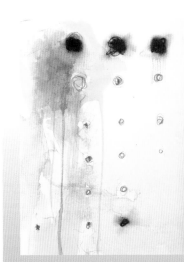

TARA CHICKEY
Memory of a Color, **2008**
7½ x 9 inches (19 x 22.9 cm);
handmade book; silkscreen, ink,
watercolors PHOTO BY ARTIST

Album Cover

An Album Cover is similar to a full-case binding cover in that both are made of book board. Also in both, the covering material forms the joint between the boards.

GWEN DIEHN **Untitled, 2009**
7 x 8 x ½ inches (17.8 x 20.3 x 1.3 cm); Album binding

WHAT YOU NEED

Bookbinding Tool Kit (page 47)

2 pieces of Davey board or mat board, each cut to ¼ inch (6 mm) wider and taller than the text pages

2 pieces of paper, thin leather, or book cloth, each 2 inches (5.1 cm) wider and taller than the boards

1 or 2 (for a fold-over cover) piece(s) of strong paper, such as mulberry, or a piece of light cloth, such as mull or netting, 2 inches (5.1 cm) x the height of the cover board

2 pieces of end paper, ¼ inch (6 mm) shorter and less wide than the cover boards

Scrap wood at least as big as the closed book

Power or hand drill with a ¼-inch (6 mm) or ⅜-inch (1 cm) bit

2 rags: 1 damp and 1 dry

WHAT YOU DO

MAKING A TRADITIONAL ALBUM COVER

1 On the *front* cover board, draw a vertical line 1½ inch (3.8 cm) in from the left (or spine) edge. Cut the board along the line and lay the cut piece aside. Mark a new vertical line on the larger piece of board exactly ¼ inch (6 mm) in from the same edge (figure 1, page 126).

2 Cut away the ¼-inch (6 mm) strip. You'll use this narrow piece of board as a spacer between the 1½-inch (3.8 cm) spine and the rest of the cover. This space allows the album to open fully. If the space is too narrow, the cover cannot fold back.

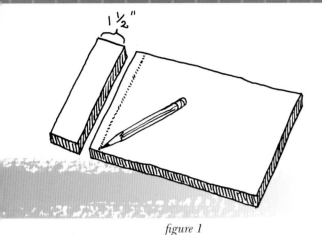

figure 1

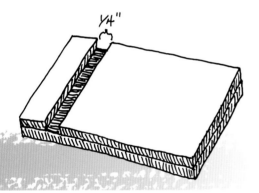

figure 2

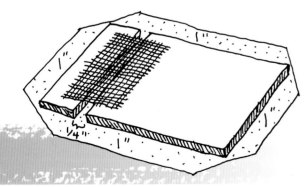

figure 3

3 Place the smaller spine piece of board beside the larger piece on top of the uncut back cover, using the ¼-inch (6 mm) strip cut in step 2 to hold the space. Remove the strip of board. The two covers should be the exact same size, allowing for the ¼-inch (6 mm) gap on the front cover (figure 2).

4 Before covering the boards, read Preventing Warped Boards (see Bookbinding Essentials). Then center the back cover on the wrong side of one sheet of covering material (paper, thin leather, or book cloth). You should have a 1-inch (2.5 cm) glue tab around each side. Refer to the Bookbinding Essentials for the next steps to cover the back cover board.

5 Cover the front board exactly as you did the back, while maintaining the ¼-inch (6 mm) gap between the spine board and the larger board. Before covering the board, lay the piece of strong paper or light cloth over the gap (figure 3). Glue it to both boards and burnish it to strengthen the hinge and to hold the two boards in place relative to each other. Whenever gluing, use a damp rag and a dry rag to keep the project and your hands clean. Finish covering the front board as described in the Bookbinding Essentials. When you finish, the two covers should be exactly the same size: one solid board and one hinged board.

6 See Bookbinding Essentials to add the end papers. Brush PVA on the back of each piece and burnish it in place.

7 Return to the instructions for the Album book (page 75) to learn how to assemble the text block and covers. Use the scrap wood to protect your work surface when punching or drilling the holes in the cover.

Ledger Cover

This cover is specifically designed to protect your ledger text block. There are several different versions, and four are described here. Regardless which version you choose, use heavy cover-weight paper, such as Canson MiTientes, because this cover has to remain flexible, yet strong.

WHAT YOU NEED

Bookbinding Tool Kit (page 47)

Heavy cover-weight paper, as measured in the steps below (depending on the type of ledger cover chosen)

GWEN DIEHN **Untitled, 2005**
5 x 4 inches (12.7 x 10.2 cm);
traditional Ledger binding

WHAT YOU DO

1 Follow the directions for each type of ledger cover that appears with each of the figures.

2 To make a *traditional ledger cover* (figure 1), mark and cut the two cover papers the exact height and width of the text pages.

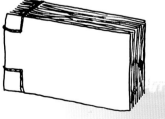

figure 1

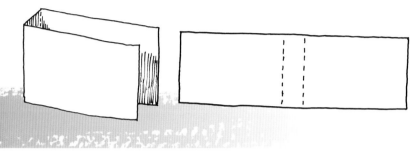

figure 2

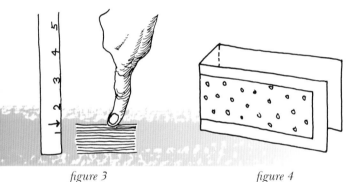

figure 3

3 To make a *spine wrapped cover* (figure 2), measure the exact height of the text pages and cut the cover to that height. For the cover's width, measure the width of the text pages, double it, and add the width of the spine. To determine the spine width, stack and gently compress all the text pages (figure 3).

4 To make a *double cover* (figure 4), first make a spine wrapped cover, as described in step 3. Then cut a second, top cover slightly smaller than the main cover (figure 5). Lay the smaller cover over the larger cover and sew it in place. You can make this cover from a simple ledger cover as well as from a spine wrapped cover.

5 To make a *foredge folds cover* (figure 6), follow step 3 to make a spine wrapped cover, except double the width of the cover—but subtract ⅛ inch (3 mm) from each doubled front and back cover (figure 7). Score the fold lines, fold the paper, and use the bone folder to flatten the folded flaps evenly. The folded flaps strengthen the cover. This is a very good cover to use if the chosen cover paper is not very heavy. As with the double cover, you can make this cover from a simple ledger cover as well as from a spine wrapped cover.

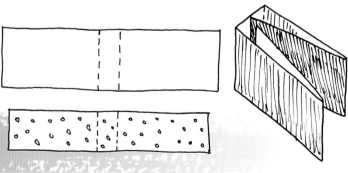

figure 4

figure 5

figure 6

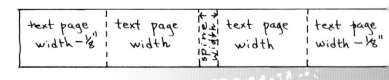

figure 7

Flexible Cover Dos-à-Dos

A *dos-à-dos* is a back-to-back double book, very useful for expressing two different voices, points of view, aspects of a project, or any other doubling. This version uses two simple Pamphlets. If you want a more substantial double book, see page 101 for a double Coptic book.

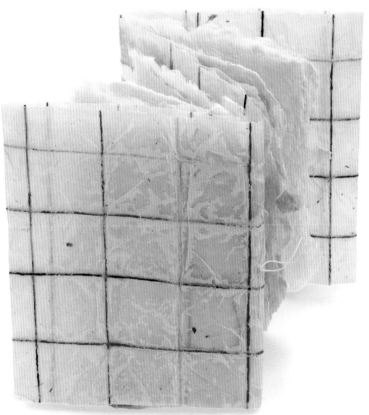

GWEN DIEHN **Unitled, 2009**
6 x 4 x 1 inches (15.2 x 10.2 x 2.5 cm); Dos-à-Dos Double Pamphlet book; cover of oiled paper with wire inlay, handmade paper pamphlets

WHAT YOU NEED

Bookbinding Tool Kit (page 47)

2 pamphlets (or signatures), folded but not yet sewn (see Bookbinding Essentials)

Heavy, cover-weight paper, as measured in step 1

Scrap paper, 2 inches (5.1 cm) x the height of the text pages

4 paper clips

3-ply bookbinder's thread

Straight needle

WHAT YOU DO

1. Trim the cover paper so it is the exact height of the pamphlets. Now trim it so that it is ⅝ inch (1.6 cm) wider than 5 times the width of one folded pamphlet or signature, as in figure 1.

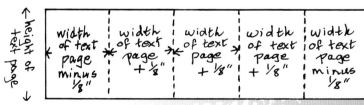

figure 1

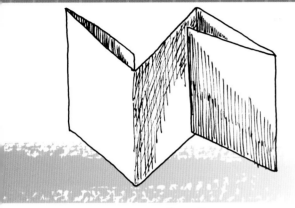

figure 2

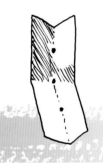

figure 3

figure 4

2 Use the bone folder and ruler to score and then fold the cover paper as in figure 2. See Bookbinding Essentials for help with scoring and folding if necessary.

3 To make a pattern for a Multiple Pamphlet book, fold the 2-inch-wide (5.1 cm) strip of scrap paper in half lengthwise. Crease the center fold, and then unfold it. Fold it in half again, this time in the other direction. Crease and unfold again. The place where the creases cross is the center point. Pencil mark that spot. Make two more marks along the lengthwise fold: 1 inch (2.5 cm) down from the top and 1 inch (2.5 cm) up from the bottom (figure 3). If your book is taller than 5 inches (12.7 cm), center additional marks between the center mark and both other (top and bottom) marks.

4 Place a pamphlet into the second fold of the cover from the left. Lift the cover and opened pamphlet, and then press them into the gutter of the opened phone book. Press the pattern on top, fitting the lengthwise crease into the gutter. See Bookbinding Essentials.

5 Use the awl to poke holes in the pamphlet and cover, according to the pattern. Secure the pamphlet to the cover using the paper clips. Sew the pamphlet to the cover following directions for a pamphlet stitch on page 73.

6 When you've sewn in the first pamphlet, turn the cover and pamphlet over to the other side of the cover. Repeat steps 4 and 5 to attach the second pamphlet. Fold the flaps in (figure 4).

Longstitch Cover

To make a Longstitch cover, you need built-in straps along the spine. These are easy to create. This cover works well with recycled light cardboard, such as a cookie box or six-pack carton, but you can also make it with heavy, cover-weight paper or leather. You can even use an old hardcover book if the spine is intact.

WHAT YOU NEED

Bookbinding Tool Kit (page 47)

Recycled carton or heavy, cover-weight paper, as measured in step 1

Alternatively, a used hardcover book that's large enough to accommodate your text block (see step 6)

GWEN DIEHN *Italy Sketchbook,* **2007**
3½ x 5½ x ½ inches (8.9 x 14 x 1.3 cm); Longstitch binding with recycled cardboard cover

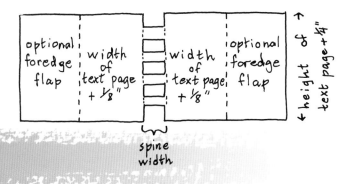

figure 1

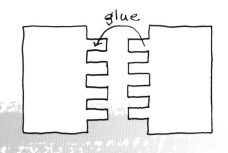

figure 2

figure 3   figure 4

WHAT YOU DO

1 Trim the cover material to fit the text block (figure 1). Cut the front and back covers to be ¼ inch (6 mm) taller than the text block and ⅛ to ¼ inch (3 to 6 mm) wider. To add foredge fold-in flaps, double the width of each cover (figure 1 again). If your cover material is too small to make both covers at once, you can make it in two parts (figure 2). To measure the spine width, stack all the signatures in order and press gently (figure 3).

2 Score and then fold the spine edges (and flaps, if you have them) represented as the dotted lines in figure 1.

3 Starting at the top edge of the cover material, draw a series of rectangles down the spine width as in figure 1. Finish with a last rectangle at the very bottom. The number of rectangles depends solely on the size of the book. You can draw an even or odd number. Leave at least ½ inch (1.3 cm) between each rectangle. These spaces will serve as the sewing straps. If you are using two pieces of cover material, mark them as in figure 2.

4 Carefully cut out the rectangles, leaving the straps. Make sure to cut the rectangles out of the very top and very bottom of the spine, as shown in figures 1 and 2. If you have two pieces of cover material, glue the straps together by brushing PVA on just the straps.

5 Instead of using cardboard or heavy paper, you can recycle an old hardcover book cover to make a Longstitch Cover. Cut through the end pages of the text block as shown in figure 4. Be careful to cut only the end papers. Leave the spine connected to the two covers. Then follow steps 3 and 4 above.

Flexible Glued-In Cover

This cover is exactly what its name implies: a piece of flexible material—such as unmounted leather, heavy cover-weight paper, or heavy canvas—to which a Sewn on Tapes, Pamphlet, Multiple Pamphlet, or Australian Reversed Piano Hinge text block is glued. This handsome, serviceable cover, especially when made with leather, holds up well on a journal subjected to constant wear and tear. To make a window in this cover (for artwork, a title, or a photograph), see page 55.

WHAT YOU NEED

Bookbinding Tool Kit (page 47)

Unmounted leather or heavy cover-weight paper (as measured in figure 1, 2, or 3)

Scrap paper

Graphite or white (for leather or dark paper) pencil

2 rags: 1 damp and 1 dry

GWEN DIEHN *Sketchbook, 2002*
3½ x 5 x 1¼ inches
(8.9 x 12.7 x 3.2 cm); Sewn on
Tapes glued into a flexible
cover with fold-over

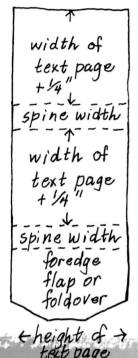

width of
text page
+ 1/4"

spine width

width of
text page
+ 1/4"

spine width
foredge
flap or
foldover

←height of→
text page
+ 1/2"

figure 1

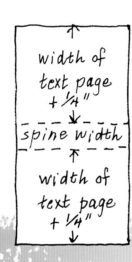

width of
text page
+ 1/4"

spine width

width of
text page
+ 1/4"

figure 2

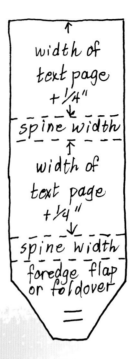

width of
text page
+ 1/4"

spine width

width of
text page
+ 1/4"

spine width
foredge flap
or foldover

figure 3

figure 4   *figure 5*   *figure 6*

WHAT YOU DO

1 Measure and cut the cover material, following the guidelines in figures 1, 2, or 3, depending on whether or not you want foredge flaps (figures 1 or 3) and/or a tie (figure 3).

2 If your text block is Sewn on Tapes, glue the tapes to the hinge before proceeding to step 3. If the style is Australian Reversed Piano Hinge, glue the end hinge to the first page of the book before proceeding. If the style has a concertina, glue the end page of the concertina to the first page of the text block. For all other binding styles, proceed directly to step 3.

3 Place a piece of scrap paper between the first text page and the element to be glued to the cover. Figure 4 shows a text block with a Sewn on Tapes binding (first the hinge is glued to the cover). Figure 5 shows a text block with an Australian Reversed Piano Hinge. Figure 6 shows a text block sewn onto a concertina, but this example also works for a Pamphlet or a Multiple Pamphlet.

figure 7

4 Brush PVA all over the surface of the outer element (the page or hinge, if the book is Sewn on Tapes). Use the rags to keep your hands and the project clean. Remove the scrap paper. Carefully position the spine and then lay the gluey element down on the cover in the desired position (figure 7). Burnish carefully with the bone folder.

figure 8

5 While holding the text block standing upright on its spine, place a piece of scrap paper between the just-glued element (hinge or page) and the rest of the text block. Gently lay the text block over onto the glued side (figure 8). Note that you have not glued the spine to the cover.

6 Repeat steps 3 and 4 to glue the other side of the text block to the cover (figure 9). Burnish thoroughly.

7 If your book has a Sewn on Tapes binding, stand the book, which you've already glued into the cover by the hinges, on its spine and place a piece of scrap paper between the first page and the rest of the text block (figure 10).

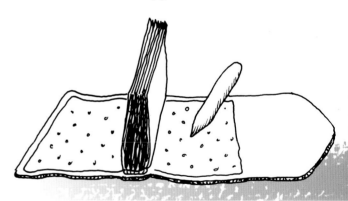

figure 9

8 Repeat step 4 to glue down the first page of the text block to the cover, hiding the hinges and finishing your book. When you've completed this step, place scrap paper between the covers and the rest of the text block and close the book to let it dry completely. Put a light weight, such as two old mint tins filled with pennies, on top of the book to press it.

figure 10

Flexible Laced-In Cover

This cover works with a Sewn on Tapes text block (with or without a concertina), as well as an Accordion Sewn on Tapes binding. A flexible laced-in cover is a nice non-adhesive cover to use with a non-adhesive binding. Two versions are presented here: a simple piece of leather with a wrap-around flap, and heavy paper with folded-in foredges.

WHAT YOU NEED

Bookbinding Tool Kit (page 47)

Flexible leather, ⅛ inch (3 mm) thick, or heavy cover-weight paper, as measured in step 1

Graphite or white pencil

GWEN DIEHN *Italy Journal,* **2007**
6 x 7 x 1 inches (15.2 x 17.8 x 2.5 cm); Sewn on Tapes binding laced into a flexible cover with fold-over and tie, leather with Israeli goat vellum tapes

WHAT YOU DO

1 Measure and cut the leather or paper as shown in figure 1. Lay the sewn text block on top of the cover (wrong side up) in the exact position you want it.

2 Mark the position of the top and bottom of each sewing tape (or strap) onto the cover material. For leather or dark colored paper, use a white pencil so it's easier to see. Draw horizontal lines on the cover to mark the top and bottom of the slits to be cut (figure 2). For paper, do not draw lines on the flaps.

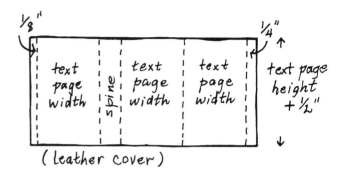

1/8"

1/4"

text page width | spine | text page width | text page width

text page height + 1/2"

(leather cover)

height of page + 1/2"

text page width minus 1/8" | text page width | spine | text page width | text page width minus 1/8"

(heavy paper)

figure 1

DANIELLE BAUMGARTNER
Untitled Journal, 2007
6 x 8 x 1 inches (15.2 x 20.3 x 2.5 cm);
cover of Twinrocker Simon's Green Rough
paper, text block sewn over leather straps
with decorative stitching on spine

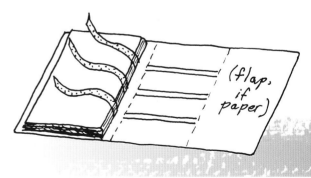

(flap, if paper)

figure 2

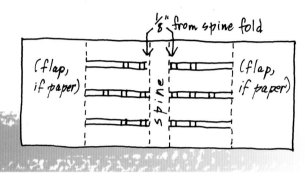

figure 3

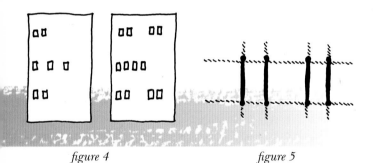

figure 4　　　　*figure 5*

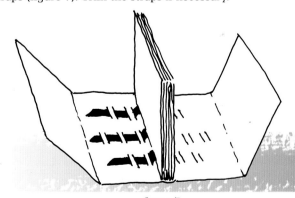

figure 6

figure 7

3 Remove the text block and draw pairs of vertical lines about ½ inch (1.3 cm) apart between the horizontal lines from step 2. These vertical lines show where to cut the lacing slits. It's a good idea to place one row of slits ⅛ inch (3 mm) from the spine (figure 3). Add at least two other rows. Since you start lacing from inside the book and you've drawn the vertical slits in pairs, the straps will always end inside the book. Draw a pleasing pattern of slits that complements the outer cover. Figure 4 shows two sample patterns.

4 Lay the cover on the cutting mat. Punch a small hole at the top and bottom of each slit-to-be. Then carefully cut the slits from hole to hole (figure 5).

5 For a paper cover, score the foredge and fold it under (figure 6).

6 Lace in the straps this way: Stand the text block in the spine of the cover, spine side down. Push the first strap—top or bottom, left or right—into the first slot. Then, from the outside of the book, push the strap into the next slot. Continue until you've laced the first strap through all its slots. Repeat this step for all the other straps (figure 7). Trim the straps if necessary.

Flexible Sewn-In Cover

This cover, which you can make with many types of materials, fits a single Pamphlet as well as Multiple Pamphlets with or without a concertina. To create an interesting cover for a yoga journal, for example, use a woven cloth placemat or try a piece of corrugated-on-one-side paper. Another good choice is a piece of soft leather.

WHAT YOU NEED

Bookbinding Tool Kit (page 47)

Chosen cover material (see Note)

Scrap paper, 2 inches (5.1 cm) x the height of the text pages

3-ply bookbinder's thread in a color that complements the cover material

Straight needle

12 paper clips

Note: A woven cloth placemat makes a perfect journal cover if you're using a relatively large page size since you can't cut the placemat material down to size; the material unravels. To find corrugated-on-one-side paper, look in craft supply, art supply, or school supply stores. Sometimes it's sold as bulletin board material.

GWEN DIEHN   **Untitled, 2009**
6 x 8 x ½ inches (15.2 x 20.3 x 1.3 cm); Multiple Pamphlets sewn directly to flexible cover, leather with beads, three-ply waxed linen thread

figure 1 (for a woven placemat)

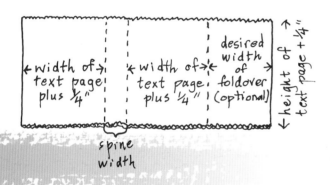

figure 2 (for corrugated paper)

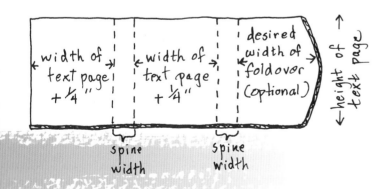

figure 3 (for leather)

WHAT YOU DO

1 Measure and cut the cover material according to figures 1, 2, or 3, depending on the chosen cover material. Cut corrugated paper and leather twice as wide as a text page, plus the width of the spine. If you want a fold-over flap, add about 2 inches (5.1 cm) more to the width. To determine the spine width needed for corrugated paper and leather covers, see figure 3 on page 132.

2 To make a pattern, fold the 2-inch-wide (5.1 cm) strip of scrap paper in half lengthwise. Crease the center fold, and then unfold it. Fold it in half again, this time in the other direction. Crease and unfold again. The place where the creases cross is the center point. Pencil mark that spot. Make two, four, or six more marks along the lengthwise fold, depending on the height of the text pages. Make these marks about 1 inch (2.5 cm) apart and at least ½ inch (1.3 cm) from the top and bottom edges (figure 4).

ADDING THE SIGNATURES

3 Open the telephone directory to a middle page. Place the cover on the phone book so that the spine lines up with the gutter. Lay the first pamphlet or signature, opened out, where you want to sew it to the cover (which depends on the number of signatures and the width of the spine). Press the pattern into the crease of the signature. Punch this row of holes, and then secure the signature with four paper clips (figure 5).

4 Thread the needle and insert it into the bottom hole from inside the signature. Pull the thread through, leaving a 4- to 5-inch (10.2 to 12.7 cm) tail. Secure the tail under one of the paperclips.

5 Sew in and out of the remaining holes as shown in figure 6, pulling the thread taut with each stitch. Although figure 6 shows a pattern for five holes, you can adapt it for three holes or for more than five by reducing or repeating the pattern as needed.

6 After sewing all holes, pull the thread to the bottom hole, where the tail is hanging. Inside the signature, tie off the tail with the sewing thread and cut the thread to ½ inch (1.3 cm).

7 Open out the next signature and place it in the cover so its center fold is as close as possible to the sewn center fold of the first signature (figure 7). Repeat steps 4 to 6 for this signature and all the remaining ones, to sew them to the cover.

8 Sew each row immediately after making it because otherwise you might have trouble lining up the cover holes with the signature holes. To solve this problem, use opened-out paper clips to mark the holes in the signature and cover material as you punch them with the awl. Remove the paper clips only just before sewing each hole.

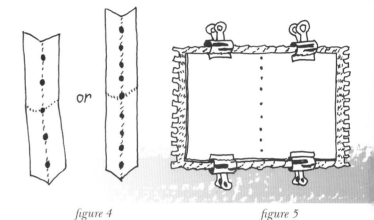

figure 4   *figure 5*

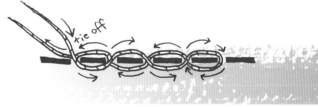

figure 6

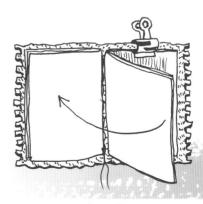

figure 7

Coptic Covers

Since a Coptic is an open-spine binding, it doesn't need a spine board, but it does require two separate cover boards. These can be hard board covers, flexible covers, or covers made of unusual materials such as metal or ceramic. Basically, you can use anything through which you can drill, punch, or fashion a hole. Here are several designs for Coptic covers.

WHAT YOU NEED

Bookbinding Tool Kit (page 47)

Piece of aluminum from the bottom of a disposable aluminum turkey roasting pan or a piece of light copper from a craft supply store

Aluminum shears or heavy scissors capable of cutting light metal

Awl or drill with a ⅛-inch (3 mm) bit suitable for metal

Scrap wood to protect work surface while drilling or punching

For Metal Covers

WHAT YOU DO

1 Cut the metal using aluminum shears so you have room for a ¼-inch (6 mm) hem on all four sides (figure 1). Be sure to trim each corner at 45°.

2 Use the ruler and bone folder to turn the hem over and flatten it down on all four edges (figure 2). Bump each pointy corner on a hard surface to flatten it slightly (figure 3).

3 If you want to make designs on the metal, use a nail or the awl to punch and engrave. See figure 4 for a sample.

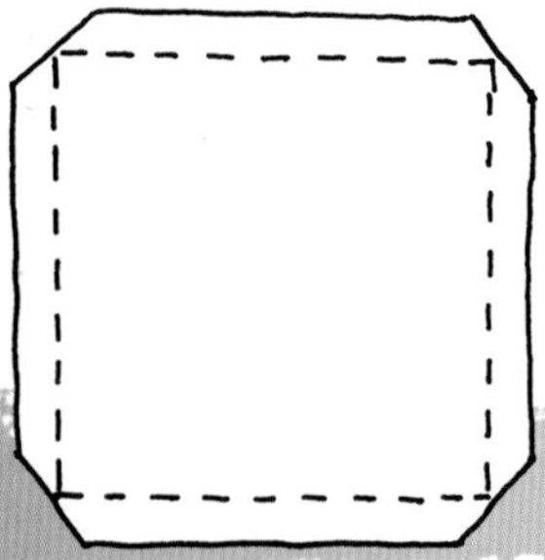

figure 1

figure 2

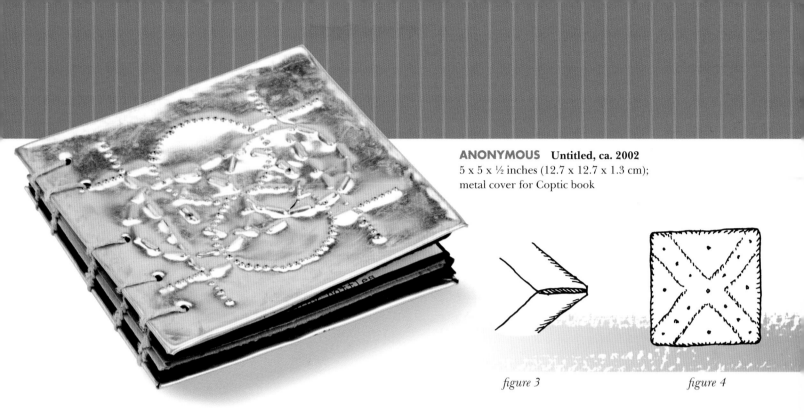

ANONYMOUS   **Untitled, ca. 2002**
5 x 5 x ½ inches (12.7 x 12.7 x 1.3 cm);
metal cover for Coptic book

figure 3   *figure 4*

4 Use the awl or drill to make sewing holes in one cover
at a time. You can use any arrangement of holes: an
even or an odd number of holes will work. Just be sure
to keep all holes at least ½ inch (1.3 cm) from all edges.
Figure 5 shows some sample patterns.

5 After drilling holes in the first cover, use it as a pattern
for the second cover. Align both covers so that they're
facing correctly for the finished book, and use the awl or
a nail to mark the hole placement on the second cover.
Remove the first cover and punch or drill the holes on
the second cover.

6 Sew the book following directions on page 98 (Coptic
binding) or 112 (Coptic with Concertina).

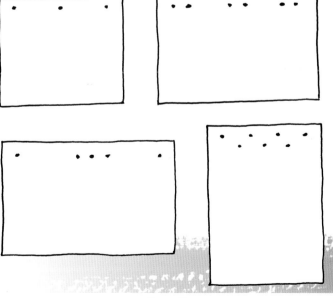

figure 5

For Hard Board Covers

GWEN DIEHN **Untitled Journal, 2009**
4½ x 6½ x ½ inches (11.4 x 15.2 x 1.3 cm);
Coptic binding with a recycled hardback book
cover and a concertina made out of a map

WHAT YOU NEED

Bookbinding Tool Kit (page 47)

*2 pieces of Davey Board, mat board, or
illustration board, big enough for the covers*

*Paper or bookcloth to cover the boards (see page
52 to make bookcloth out of regular cloth)*

*Endpapers or end pages (paper to line the
boards), cut as shown in Bookbinding Essentials*

2 rags: 1 damp and 1 dry

WHAT YOU DO

1 Read "Preventing Warped Boards" in Bookbinding
Essentials. Measure and cut the two cover boards so that
each board is ⅛ to ¼ inch (3 to 6 mm) higher and wider
than your book's signature. See Bookbinding Essentials
and follow the directions for covering boards with paper,
leather, or cloth.

2 Cut the end papers as shown in Bookbinding Essentials.
Cover opposite sides of the boards with end pages.

3 Flip to the directions for a Coptic Binding (page 98)
or a Coptic with Concertina (page 102) book. To add a
window or encrustation to a paper-covered cover, turn
to page 56. To try collage, see page 67.

For Paper-Covered Hard Boards

There is an alternate way to cover boards for a Coptic cover that results in a very lovely edge. My friend Sandy Webster learned this method while teaching in Australia and New Zealand.

WHAT YOU NEED

Bookbinding Tool Kit (page 47)

2 pieces of cover paper (which also become the lining papers), each the height of the cover plus ¼ inch (6 mm) and twice as wide plus ¼ inch (6 mm) as in figure 6

Scrap paper

2 rags: 1 damp and 1 dry

WHAT YOU DO

1 Trim each cover paper as in figure 6. Lay each piece in turn on scrap paper, and brush PVA completely over the surface of the paper. Use the rags to keep the project clean.

2 Carefully place a cover board down on the glued surface as shown in figure 6. Using the bone folder, fold the leftover paper over the board, being sure to pull the paper snug against the edge of the board. Rub the paper in place on the board and burnish it.

3 Use the bone folder to tightly burnish the overlapping edges to form a kind of crimped edge (figure 7).

4 Place the cover on the cutting surface and carefully trim the overlap to ⅛ inch (3 mm). Use the scissors to round the corners (figure 8). Repeat steps 2 through 4 for the other cover.

5 Turn to directions for a Coptic binding (page 98) or Coptic with Concertina (page 102). You can also add collage (page 67) or an encrustation (page 58) to this cover.

GWEN DIEHN
Untitled, 2008
4 x 6½ x ½ inches
(10.2 x 16.5 x 1.3 cm);
New Zealand cover on
a Three-Hole Coptic
book, with collage
of fine netting,
acrylic edges

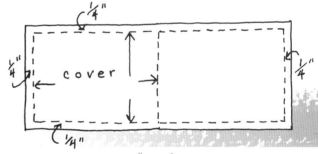

figure 6

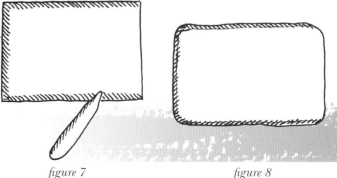

figure 7   *figure 8*

For Folded Paper Covers

GWEN DIEHN
Untitled Journal, 2009
4 x 5 x ½ inches
(10.2 x 12.7 x 1.3 cm);
folded paper cover for
Coptic book

WHAT YOU NEED

Bookbinding Tool Kit (page 47)

2 pieces of heavy paper to use for both the cover and the cover liner, each twice as wide as the cover plus 2 inches (5.1 cm) x as high as the cover plus 2 inches (5.1 cm)

WHAT YOU DO

1 Trim each sheet of the cover paper as shown in figure 9. Score the fold lines.

2 Fold along all the score lines and assemble each cover (figures 10 and 11). One side edge of each cover is a fold, while the other side edge creates a slot into which you insert the tab. Be sure to punch the sewing holes along the slot and tab edges so that the folded edges become the foredges of the book.

3 Turn to the directions for a Coptic binding (page 98) or Coptic with Concertina (page 102).

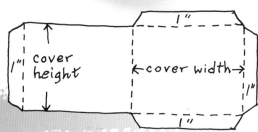

figure 9

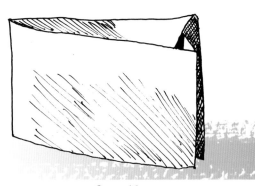

figure 10

figure 11

Full-Case Hardback Cover

This closed-spine cover offers maximum protection to a text block. It works well with a Sewn on Tapes binding (with or without a concertina), as well as an Accordion Sewn on Tapes binding, a Multiple Pamphlet, or an Australian Reversed Piano Hinge binding. You can also use it for a double book. Cover it with paper, cloth, or very thin leather.

WHAT YOU NEED

Bookbinding Tool Kit (page 47)

Paper, cloth, or thin leather, cut as shown in Bookbinding Essentials

3 pieces of archival cardboard, such as Davey board, as measured in step 1

Scrap paper

2 rags: 1 damp and 1 dry

GWEN DIEHN **Untitled Journal, 2006**
5 x 5 x 1 inches (12.7 x 12.7 x 2.5 cm);
Sewn on Tapes book with a headband
and a full-case hard cover

figure 1

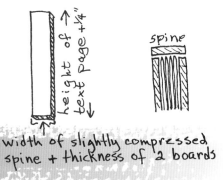

figure 2

figure 3   figure 4

WHAT YOU DO

PREPARING THE COVER BOARDS

1 Cut the archival cardboard into two equal pieces to be the front and back covers, as shown in figure 1. Cut a third piece of archival cardboard to be the spine, as in figure 2.

2 Lay the cloth, paper, or leather wrong side up on top of the scrap paper. Assemble the two cover boards and the spine board as explained in Bookbinding Essentials. Mark the cloth, paper, or leather to show the correct placement of the boards. Be sure to maintain a ¼-inch (6 mm) gap between cover boards and spine.

3 Follow the directions in Bookbinding Essentials for covering boards with paper, leather, paper-lined book cloth, or unlined book cloth. Pay attention to the corner details.

JOINING THE TEXT BLOCK TO THE COVER

4 If your book has a binding other than a Sewn on Tapes binding, skip to step 7. Otherwise, glue the binding tapes to the pages next to them. Slip the scrap paper under both end pages of the text block. Brush PVA on the tapes and press the tapes to the page (figure 3).

5 Slip scrap paper under one of the hinge flaps and brush PVA onto the outside of the hinge flap (figure 4).

6 Carefully center the spine on the spine board. Hold the text block so it stands straight up while you burnish the hinge flap to the board (figure 5).

7 Repeat steps 5 and 6 for the other hinge flap.

8   Slip scrap paper under the first end page with the sewing tapes glued to it—or under the first inside cover page, if the book doesn't have a Sewn on Tapes binding—and brush PVA all over the surface, including any tapes.

9   Holding the spine of the text block flat against the spine board, fold the gluey page flat down and burnish it with your finger to the inside of the first cover board. Use your finger to *gently* push the paper into the gap between spine and cover. This is a very important step. Do *not* stretch the paper across the gap, or the book will not open properly. Instead, push the end paper down into the gap to maintain the gap and its flexibility. Use your fingers, as a bone folder could tear the damp paper. Repeat for the other end page (figure 6).

FINISHING THE BOOK

10   Note that the spine itself is not glued to the spine board. The spine must remain loose and flexible so that the book can open and close. After burnishing the end pages (being mindful of the gaps), lay pieces of scrap paper between each cover and the text block. Carefully close the book and lay it down on one side.

11   Use your fingers to press the covering material (the cloth, paper, or leather) into the groove between the spine and the covers on both sides. Note that the spine board should slightly overlap the cover boards (figure 7).

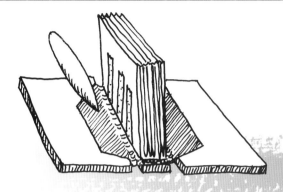

figure 5

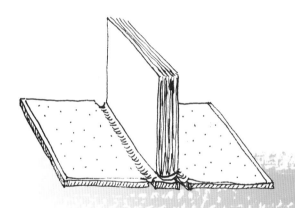

figure 6

figure 7

journals
past + present

When you become part of the community of journal keepers, you may find that you want to learn more about the fascinating history of this long-practiced activity that is still vital today. The profiles in this chapter will give you a taste of what others are doing now. You'll also read about some remarkable journal keepers from the past. After the profiles, you'll find a gallery of real life journal pages to further inspire you.

Not Your Average Memory Book

Like anything else that isn't used regularly, memory can easily lose its sharpness and strength. In the not-so-distant past, people exercised their memory daily, and in the more distant past they deliberately cultivated and strengthened it with approaches that ranged from simple to amazingly elaborate. Among my favorites in the elaborate category is the construction of memory palaces.

Memory Palaces & Wax Tablets

Ancient Greek orators were trained to memorize the structure of their arguments and metaphors by constructing mental palaces and then furnishing them with visually distinct features, such as columns and nooks, tables and benches. To each of the furnishings or features they were to attach sentences, which they could retrieve by mentally moving through the house to the appropriate place, where they could scoop up the sentence hanging from the mantelpiece or the argument draped over the bench. A memory house needed to be re-furnished with new metaphors and arguments for each occasion, and the orator's agility at moving through the rooms and retrieving the appropriate arguments and sentences increased with experience.

At the other end of the spectrum of early mnemonic devices was the kinesthetic practice of teaching young students to read by having them trace the words on wax tablets with a stylus, thus causing the words to become a part of the student's sense of touch. Think for a moment of the sensory difference between tapping on a keyboard and the sinuous dance of a pen on slightly toothy paper as it forms cursive writing.

Commonplace Books

Memory, of course, is more than just the ability to retrieve facts quickly, and as early as the 13th century, people recognized that memory was crucial to the process of mental digestion of what had been read. The keeping of a notebook, which later came to be called a *commonplace book*, was considered the next step after reading

and digesting what was read. Scholars were urged to write down the pithiest statements from what they read and keep them in blank books organized by predetermined headings so they could easily refer to them when needed.

During the Renaissance, the practice was adapted to suit pedagogical needs. Humanist teachers, such as Erasmus, wrote manuals with detailed instructions for commonplacing. The wonderful Latin word *florilegiae* was used to describe this gathering of "flowers" of *sententiae* (wise, moralistic, and memorable sayings extracted from longer works). Readers were urged to amass personal collections of *florilegiae*. The point wasn't to be original, but to glean from every available source the most pithy and important ideas and sayings, and the most uplifting images. The process of rewording and working with recently read ideas imprinted them on the reader's memory, and the commonplace book itself was given a didactic function when it was shared with friends.

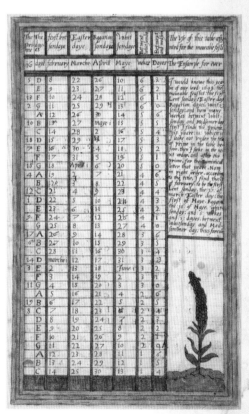

THOMAS TREVELYON
Trevelyon Miscellany (Page 18r), **1608**
11 x 17 inches (27.9 x 43.2 cm);
by permission of the Folger
Shakespeare Library

151

Thomas Trevelyon's *Miscellany*

A related practice was that of compiling a *miscellany*, a collection of articles and images on various subjects into a single volume. The organizing principle was the compiler's own interests and what he or she considered morally uplifting and useful.

Thomas Trevelyon's *Miscellany* of 1608 is just such a collection, a gathering of fragments, reminiscent of Erasmus's image of bees collecting pollen and bringing it to their hives. In fact, it's the largest, most colorful, most multimedia book of this genre, densely packed with edifying statements, history, chronology, the science of the day, design ideas, religion, moralistic statements, practical knowledge, and exhortations to virtuous living. The book weighs 17 lbs and has 654 pages of hand-written text and hand-drawn images. Trevelyon drew his text and images from popular sources of the day, and the book is thus an extraordinary time capsule of life in the time of Shakespeare. Many of the original works from which he gleaned his *florilegiae* are no longer extant, making the *Miscellany* the only source we have for these works.

In Trevelyon's England, people believed in preparing for the future by learning the lessons of the past; faith in a merciful god gave them confidence and some comfort against the uncertainties of life. Commonplace books and miscellanies were collections of the wisdom of the times, intended for personal pleasure as well as for the edification of friends. Both image and text triggered memory of pious and uplifting thoughts and stories. Familiarity, not originality, was the point. People recognized the iconography in these books because it appeared on church facades, in books of hours, and emblem books.

Trevelyon mined prose and verse, engravings and woodcuts for his articles and imagery, changing them freely to suit his lively and engaging page designs. Before the advent of rigid individual authorship, let alone individual intellectual property and copyright, the social construction of knowledge held sway, and it was expected that a writer or printmaker would build on the best of common knowledge. The following list of some of Trevelyon's topics gives a good indication of his broad interests and what he considered most edifying and useful to share with his friends:

Verse maxims on household management
A brief computation of the time complete within the present year
Proverbs
The seven deadly sins
A wife's duties to her husband
The Muses
Verse maxims on husbandry and the stages of life
How a man may journey from any notable town in England to the city of London
The creation of the world
A history of England
The seven virtuous women
An almanac
Design motifs, patterns, and alphabets (139 in all)

Happily for us, it is possible to see and even handle Trevelyon's *Miscellany*. The original manuscript, part of the collection of the Folger Shakespeare Library in Washington, D.C., is too fragile to be handled, but the Library has published a magnificent facsimile edition, available for purchase or for your perusal in their gift shop. You can also learn more about Trevelyon's *Miscellany* at www.folger.edu.

THOMAS TREVELYON *Trevelyon Miscellany (Page 208v)*, **1608**
11 x 17 inches (27.9 x 43.2 cm); by permission of the Folger Shakespeare Library

Real Life Sketchbooks

Artists use their sketchbooks in many different ways and to fulfill a variety of purposes. The sketchbook practices of Leonardo da Vinci, Louise Bourgeois, and Oscar Bluemner demonstrate three specific approaches.

Leonardo da Vinci

Leonardo da Vinci (1452–1519), whose notebooks are legendary, used drawing as a way to learn and understand the world around him. Although he was an uneducated man—there is no record of his ever having attended a university—his unstoppable curiosity and wide-ranging intellect drove him to explore many disciplines.

Da Vinci drew dissected cadavers to improve his understanding of anatomy; he made mechanical drawings of civil engineering projects of his own invention; he drew the most important buildings of his time to study the aesthetics of architecture; he sketched designs for a flying machine centuries before the Wright brothers were even born. His sketchbooks have been called "visual commonplace books," and they are filled with the images, principles, and information with which he developed his mind. He also used his sketchbooks for planning and experimenting. They show the rudimentary ideas that he later incorporated into his paintings and designs.

Oscar Bluemner

German-born American Modernist painter Oscar Bluemner (1867–1938) came to painting after a 20-year career in architecture. His sketchbooks show the influence of architectural sketching and analysis. Inspired by the relationship of architectural forms to the landscape, Bluemner often walked in the countryside, sketchbook in hand, making broad-stroked drawings of masses and planes, light and shadow, and detailed color notes and diagrams.

He studied and then discussed in his diaries the color theory of Johann Wolfgang von Goethe (better known for his dramatic poem *Faust*), which examined how people perceive color phenomena. Bluemner was, however, most interested in the emotional and psychological impact of color in a painting. For example, Bluemner thought the color red symbolized power and energy. He even coined a pseudonym for himself: The Vermillionaire.

Bluemner wrote down his ideas and made sketches in his diaries from 1911 until 1936. Many of these entries led directly to his paintings. He specified the colors he'd use in each painting; explained his painting techniques in detail; analyzed his art; and presented his

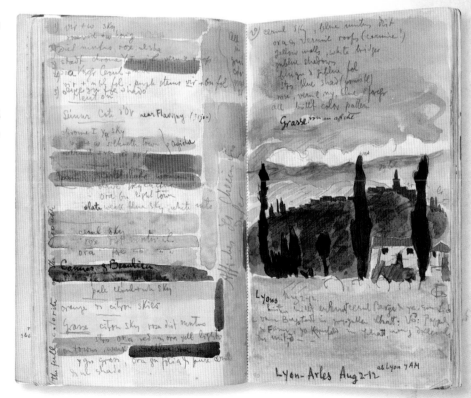

OSCAR F. BLUEMNER *Bluemner Sketchbook,* 1912
8¼ x 5⁵⁄₁₆ x ⁹⁄₁₆ inches (21 x 13.5 x 1.4 cm); sketchbook with 156 drawings in various media and artist's note on wove paper. Image courtesy of the Board of Trustees, National Gallery of Art, Washington, Gift of the Dr. Cyrus Katzen Foundation, 1999.89.1./BV

thoughts about form, color, line, palettes, creativity, and even the role of the artist. In his 1911 Painting Diary, Bluemner wrote, "One Rule: draw and paint, equally, constantly, separately, thinking, feeling." (Painting diary, 1911. Oscar Bluemner Papers, Archives of American Art, microfilm roll 339, frame 160.)

Louise Bourgeois

Contemporary artist Louise Bourgeois (born in 1911 in France), by contrast, works from the inside out in her sketchbooks. She began keeping a diary in 1923, at age 12, and kept one until 2004, when she was in her late 80s. She works with three kinds of diaries: one she writes in, another she speaks into (a tape recorder), and a third she draws in.

Her drawing diaries, which she considers the most important, reflect a practice that is from the inside out. Her drawing practice is one of discovering and giving material form to her feelings. Rather than use her diaries to record the visible world, Bourgeois draws and writes in them with a kind of automatic writing and drawing to capture her feelings and make them part of the visible world. She eventually turns some of these sketches and entries into sculptures and installations, but the diaries are not plan books for her work.

As she explained to journalist Ralf Beil in an interview in 1996: "When I draw it means something bothers me, but I don't know what it is. So it [drawing] is the treatment of anxiety. It is the transfer from anxiety to fear, the conversion… The anxiety is not defined, but then if you make a drawing suddenly you see what you are afraid of… If you have a fear you can do something about it… The drawings are not illustration, they are a conversion." (Interview with Ralf Beil, *Neue Zürcher Zeitung*, June 1996, quoted on page 111 in *Louise Bourgeois*, a catalog retrospective organized by the Tate Modern, 2008, edited by Frances Morris.)

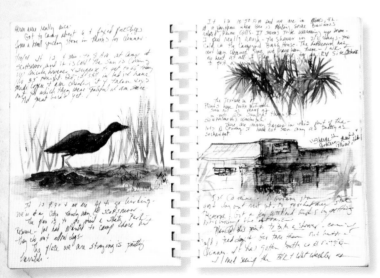

ELIZABETH ELLISON *Florida Travels* page in
September 15 '00–June 12 '01, **2001**
12½ x 12½ inches (31.8 x 31.8 cm); color-sketched
purchased journal; watercolors, pen, ink

JULIE WAGNER **Untitled, 1997**
12 x 17¼ x ¾ inches (30.5 x 43.8 x 1.9 cm); all-media sketchbook;
watercolors, ink on Canson paper PHOTO BY ARTIST

Daniel Smiley's Practice

Early naturalists and amateur scientists demonstrated how keeping records of what we observe can result in increased understanding of the subject being documented. It's hard to separate Henry David Thoreau from his journal, later published as *Walden*. The journal provided the practice, the repository, and the memory for his observations. And the very word "journal" (from the French *journée* or day) underlines the need for the everydayness of such a practice.

Daniel Smiley (1907–89) spent his life journaling about the natural world. He was the descendent of two Quaker brothers who founded a 19th century resort, Mohonk Mountain House, sequestered in 7,500 acres of farm and forest land in the Northern Shawangunk Mountains, about 90 miles north of New York City. Smiley lived at Mohonk Lake for most of his life, and spent more than 60 years as a self-trained naturalist immersed in the place, learning its every corner, and observing subtle changes in plants and animals. He also took the daily weather readings that were begun by his ancestors at Mohonk on January 1, 1896, when the Mohonk House was designated an official cooperative weather station of the U.S. Weather Bureau and outfitted with the same equipment that is used there today.

A Mountain of Note Cards

Smiley's two parallel practices—his weather recordings and his phenological observations—resulted in some 15,000 note cards at the time of his death in 1989, a collection of data that has been called "one of the most detailed long-term portraits of an ecosystem anywhere in the world." (Patrick Huyghe, "A Naturalist Preserved," *The Sciences*, NY Academy of Sciences, July–August, 1991, pp. 12–15.) *Phenology* is the ancient field study of naturally occurring phenomena, such as the first sound of spring peepers or the date of first budding of red maple trees in spring.

A typical day for Smiley would begin early in the morning when he could be seen, wearing an old green hat and a plaid jacket, walking from his home "The Elms" to the Mountain House, noting his observations along the way. His tasks each day included checking

DANIEL SMILEY RESEARCH CENTER *Paul Huth (left) and Daniel Smiley (right) inspect a Hemlock branch at Messy Point,* **1986** Courtesy of the Daniel Smiley Research Center of the Mohonk Preserve PHOTO BY GERD LUDWIG

Fishing in Winter

Daddy and I fish through the ice.
I have made a picture of the lake and where the tip-ups are.
I have made a picture of a tip-use with the hole in the ice with the line in it.
A pickerel on the hook and we have caught 10 pickerel this winter.

Daniel Smiley Jr.
Jan. 26, 1916.

DANIEL SMILEY
Letter to grandparents, **1916**
Courtesy of the Daniel Smiley
Research Center of the
Mohonk Preserve

minimum and maximum temperatures for the previous 24 hours at the weather box, checking the 1896 brass rain gauge if there had been any precipitation, making his natural history recordings in a small pocket notebook, and then recording everything in detail on their appropriate cards.

He would stop frequently to carefully note and describe what he saw, heard, or smelled. He would peek into a bird's nest partially hidden in the crevice of a rock and note that there were only two eggs in the nest that day, whereas the day before there had been four. He would jot down a line about some scat on a ledge below the nest. One of his note cards, dated 5–22–30, reads: "Eastern Chipmunk a large male chipmunk was killed by a barn cat this afternoon. Found in nest uninjured except for ears bitten. Its pouches were full of oats and some grains were still in its mouth. Subspecies identification was attempted but without success. It was said that this cat had killed 5 others the same afternoon. D.S.Jr."

His Contribution to Science

Because Smiley detected changes over time, he was aware of the increase and decrease of certain species, as well as the increasing acidity of precipitation and lake water. In 1971, Smiley joined scientists from the U.S. Department of the Interior in taking the pH of Mohonk Lake waters. He used this practice to test samples of area springs and nearly 100 episodes of precipitation a year. His collection of data and notes from this study constitutes one of the longest records of its kind in the country. This data helped scientists understand the effect of acid rain; the integration of introduced species, such as the gypsy moth, into an ecosystem; and the effect of climate change on insects, migratory and over-wintering birds, plant bloom and distribution, and seasonal animal activity.

Daniel Smiley's work is carried on today by his long-time assistant, Paul Huth, who continues the daily weather, and phenological observations with his colleagues. Huth oversees the data entry from Smiley's index cards into a computer database, but he intends to hold onto the index cards, too. In this instance, it's not a cliché to say that Huth will follow in Smiley's footsteps, since he intends to record his own observations in the same, conventional manner, following the same routes Smiley tread over the eight decades of his life. Huth maintains that "The computer can organize data, but the other language on these cards makes it alive; you can interpret it." (Larry E. Burgess, *Daniel Smiley of Mohonk: A Naturalist's Life*, NY: Purple Mountain Press, 1996, page 123.)

From Ships' Logs to Crop Books

Years ago I co-taught a college class with a teacher who decided to use a class sign-in book as a tool to create community. We commissioned a lovely book from a bookbinder, large enough for all 16 students to be able to sign in and perhaps write comments on each page.

At first the book signing was a bit of a nuisance—we had to remind students to sign in, and they seemed to regard it as a kind of time clock that could be punched and then ignored. Then one day a student strolled in and announced that she felt *wonderful*, and she wanted to make a drawing instead of just signing in. A few people gathered around, curious to watch her make her little sketch, and a few of the onlookers made drawings of their own in the book.

Gradually more and more students began to write little verses or make sketches, and once the content of the pages became more interesting, everyone took time to read what her classmates had written or drawn. We gave the book a place of honor on a pedestal.

By the end of the semester, we were using the book as a cumulative history of our class, of insights people had into the material, of questions they wanted us to follow up on, and even of plans they had for their final projects. We took photographs of projects and glued them to the pages. The other teacher and I referred to the book to take the pulse of the class, as well as to keep up with students' projects and interests. The book played a definite role in shaping the group, as well as the class itself. On the last day, everyone wrote farewell messages in the book.

Community Garden Book

A community garden doesn't require quite as much detailed information be shared among its members as a ship at sea. Nevertheless, it's a natural place to plant a group journal. I recently visited a community garden and watched various workers making notes on a clipboard full of curling, smudged papers that hung from a nail in the garden shed. There were lists of things to do and things needed, as well as dates of first flowering and the sprouting of plants. Seed packets were clipped to some pages and sketches of trellis plans or new bed designs illuminate some of the pages.

BROOKLYN BOTANIC GARDEN *Detail of crop report listing amount and type of produce picked by participants in the Brooklyn Botanic Garden Children's Garden programs,* **1929** Children's Garden Papers, Special Collections, Brooklyn Botanic Garden

Group Books for the Brooklyn Botanic Garden

The Brooklyn Botanic Garden has had a children's garden program since 1914, started by a young teacher named Ellen Eddy Shaw. In that first year, each of some 150 children was given a 5 x 7-foot (1.5 x 2.1 m) garden plot to plan, plant, tend, and harvest. In addition, each child helped out with the common area, which included the flower borders and beds of large crops, such as corn and melons.

Early in the program, the children were taught to keep journals that they called "Crop Books" to detail their harvests, expenditures for such things as seeds, and the income they derived from selling the produce.

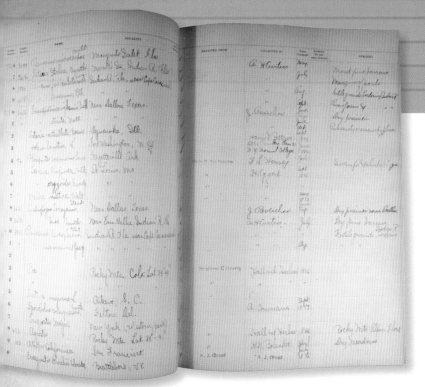

BROOKLYN BOTANIC GARDEN
Entries in ledger of herbarium accessions 1–5000
Shelved in Herbarium, Brooklyn Botanic Garden

Using the crop book introduces each child to the economics of gardening and serves as a focus that would be missing if seeds simply appeared and crops were harvested but not counted. The crop books add another layer to the experience of the gardening program and at the same time provide historical records.

The Brooklyn Botanic Garden itself has kept accession books of all plants introduced into the gardens since its inception in 1910. These books serve as a commonly kept record. The labeled columns specify the kind of information that needs to be entered by the various people responsible for receiving plants over the years. How do these books shape the experience of the group? They are a gentle reminder of what to pay attention to when new plants arrive. They represent an agreement among the people handling plants to focus on these aspects and to create a history of plant accession for future reference.

Ships' Logbooks

Books have been shaping group behavior in interesting ways for centuries. Among the earliest group books were ships' logbooks. Named for the actual log that was originally pulled behind a ship by a knotted rope as a primitive way of measuring the ship's speed, the ship's logbook was the book in which information taken from the log itself was recorded. Today, ships no longer tow actual logs, but logbooks continue to be used to record information from each crewmember's watch. A U.S. Navy ship's logbook, or deck log, is considered a legal document. Scientists also use logbook entries to study changes in the earth's magnetic poles, among other phenomena.

The preprinted categories in a logbook make certain that mariners who are entering information pay close attention to a set of conditions that have been deemed crucial in the operation of the ship. For Navy ships, the list is specified by the Office of the Chief of Naval Operations and includes the following categories:

Accidents (both material and personal injuries)
Actions (combat)
Appearance of sea/atmosphere/unusual objects
Arrests/suspensions
Bearings (navigational)
Collisions/grounding
Courts martial/captain's masts
Deaths
Honors/ceremonies/visits
Inspections
Meteorological phenomena
Movement (getting under way, course, speed changes, mooring, anchoring)
Passengers
Prisoners (crew members captured by hostile forces)
Ship's behavior (under different weather or sea conditions)
Soundings (depth of water)
Speed change
Tactical formation

Mark Combs & Otto Probst: Capturing Life's Moments

If some journal keeping can be likened to skimming for experiences with a fine net, the two journal keepers in this profile should win awards for the fineness of their nets and the duration of their skimming.

Otto Probst

Otto Probst kept journals from the age of 27 until his death at 96. Otto had a degree in engineering, which might account for the technical and factual nature of so many of his journals. He worked for 42 years as the Elkhart District Manager for the Indiana and Michigan Electric Company. He was also an avid golfer and a well-known collector of golf memorabilia. Otto referred to his several kinds of journals as his "records." They are, indeed, extremely detailed accounts of every single expenditure and dollar of income he earned throughout his adult life, as well as every event of every day—including the weather and the time the postman stopped by.

DAILY RECORDS

I got to know Otto when he was in his 80s. At that time he lived with his wife in the house in which he had been raised, a beautiful, tottering old brick stack of rooms and porches, and an attic straight out of a Nancy Drew mystery. I was a graduate student at the time and Otto's house was the subject of a paper I was writing on a historical house. I had spent several mornings measuring and sketching floor plans and talking to Otto about what the house had been like in earlier times. I noticed that sometimes he would pop out of the room and come back in consulting a small book in his hand. "Well, that window was actually added to the house in June of 1930 when we put in the downstairs bathroom. Let me see—the wood for the frame cost 76 cents, and Tom Ackerman did the work, for which we paid him—$5.20. The glass was another 30 cents."

One day I arrived to find him standing outside next to his ancient car, scrabbling through an old fruitcake tin filled with hundreds of keys. "I locked my key in the car," he explained, "but I think there's a spare in here." I offered to break into the car with a coat hanger, a skill I had acquired because of so often locking my own keys in my old VW, and

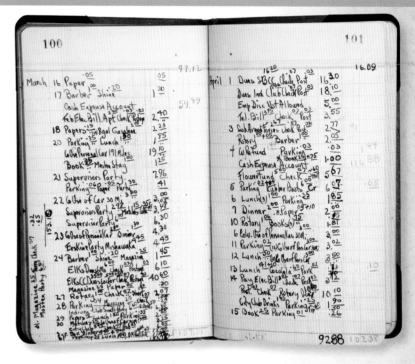

he watched with open admiration as I wiggled the hanger through a crack at the top of the window and fished up the door lock. He told me to wait right there while he went inside for a minute. He came out with one of his little black leatherette-covered record books in his hand. "I'm making an entry in my records here," he explained. "I'm writing that at 11:00 on Tuesday, February 2, 1981, you came to my house and opened my car with a coat hanger!"

When we went back inside, he showed me his collection of record books. There were shelves full of them, each book carefully labeled with the year. Some of them were of a very detail-oriented, straightforward, daily diary type—a recording of the day's minutiae: the weather, what he ate for breakfast, what time he left on an errand and what that errand entailed. Other books were more like ledgers, with entries of all his financial transactions every day of the year, including many entries for gifts bought. I loved reading that in January of 1929 he gave his little sister—my mother-in-law—a hair ornament ($1.50) for her birthday, and that other expenditures that day included 50 cents for a Charlie Chaplin movie and 35 cents for forget-me-nots.

CAR RECORDS

My favorites among these journals are his car record books. One is labeled "R. Otto Probst, South Bend, Indiana, 8 August 1936, Buick Convertible Coupe, 1 June 1936 Buick" and is covered in pebble-textured heavy black paper. The bill of sale for the car ($750 on August 11, 1936) is folded and carefully pasted on the first page of the book. The next entry is a complete technical description of the car—model number, bore and stroke of each piston, firing order of the pistons, air pressure in the tires, distributor point opening, spark plug gap, clutch pedal lash and free movement—and these are only a few of the items listed. After the initial pages the entries grow slightly more personal. Otto describes the first time he saw the car:

August 7, 1936: Had an evening off. Harry Poulin caught me just right and demonstrated a Convertible Coupe Buick 1936 Model 146C. Drove and tried it 15 minutes. Quoted $750 and my car. 3510 [odometer reading]

The rest of the book documents the date, time, destination, miles traveled, cost of fuel, and the cost of any repairs for every trip, as well as who accompanied him. On days when Otto didn't drive the car himself, the entry reads "car idle" or sometimes "John had car."

I wonder if Otto suspected at the time he was compiling his daily records that his archives would one day give people such a detailed picture of life in the early and mid-20th century. I would love to be able to talk with him today about what these records had meant to him both at the time he wrote them and as he looked back through them years later.

Mark Combs

Mark has served as the Public Works Director for the City of Asheville, North Carolina, for 14 years. He's an amateur photographer, woodworker, gardener, and skilled picture framer. In his spare time he enjoys puttering at various projects, such as working on his 1966 MGB sports car. He's raised four children and enjoys the companionship of his family and many pets.

TRACKING A DECADE OF FAMILY LIFE

Mark, another fine-net skimmer, kept a remarkable daily journal for 10 years. In the past he attempted to keep several journals with no long-term success. His great longitudinal journal was launched when his mother gave him a 10-year journal as a Christmas gift in 1996. In his earlier journals, Mark said, he had the misconceived notion that "…it was necessary to write profound thoughts and feelings so that future readers would think `Wow, what a modern-day Confucius!'" He said he quickly ran out of profound thoughts and quietly abandoned each of these early journals. But when his mother gave him the 10-year journal, Mark made a shift in his notion about journal keeping. He explained:

"Each page had four lines for 10 successive years. I thought to myself, 'Surely I can write something profound in four lines per day?' But as January 1 of the first year loomed, I thought about my earlier attempts and failures and resolved to focus on the day's events such as: Who did what, what happened, and what small thing was notable in my mind? I quickly found that this approach took the pressure off me (to be a profound philosopher!). Doing the entries quickly became an enjoyable ritual (which nib, which ink, what to write in the four lines). I found it necessary to dutifully make an entry each evening or I would forget the prior days' activities and have to concentrate to remember them! Also, after a couple of years worth of entries I found myself reading what had happened on that particular day in the past. The routine of my own life (and family) suddenly had another life on the written page. The small pieces of information I had recorded opened up a flood of memories about each event. The journal became my best friend."

One of Mark's favorite journal-keeping activities is taking photographs documenting the family's activities over time, which he would often put in the journal with descriptions. He likes to use colored inks and calligraphy, as well as small sketches. In fact, his collection of new and antique inks and fountains pens fills a large desk drawer.

ANNOTATED CALENDAR

In addition to his personal journal, before the age of electronic scheduling swept him up, Mark kept a calendar-like journal that documented appointments and activities in his job. This journal-calendar helped Mark discover a lovely way to integrate his work and family life. At first glance, a typical page in his work journal looks like a pre-printed commercial engagement calendar. Closer inspection reveals that every mark on the page, including the lines that divide the page into small sections for each day, was hand-drawn by Mark. The journal format is a clever facsimile, filled with Mark's detailed and artful writing and drawings.

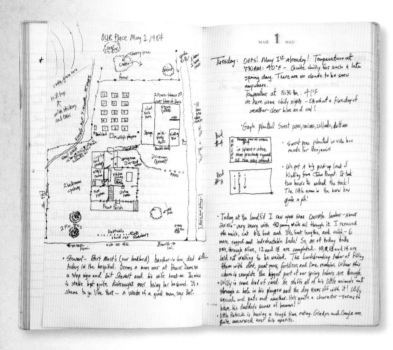

The January page, for example, has a photograph of the Combs family at the top of the page next to a colored ink painting of a smiling quarter moon in a wintry sky. He also added an antique fountain pen, a few abstract flowers, and ornate borders. Some days have colored ink sketches and designs that transform bland entries such as "Tree Commission Meeting" into opportunities for playful riffs. The weekends are also filled in, and entries like "paint hallway" and "NFL Playoffs—sewing, cooking, etc."—afford a nice balance to "Mandatory Sexual Harassment Training on the 6th Floor of City Hall at 12:30."

Mark says that he made entries in his homemade work calendar for one year, working on it in the evenings. "The journal was always in use and kept me connected to my family when I was at work," he remembered. "And comments from staff and citizens who saw it were fun too." I asked Mark what else his journals meant to him. His response was that they gave him perspective regarding "how we humans tend to look at the past through 'rose-colored glasses' and forget all the hassles and sadness that is part of all of our lives. It's human nature to block out bad memories and disasters, but the journal tells it all, including the bad times, which due to space restrictions were recorded in a pragmatic, factual way. When I read the journal, these stressful events do not cause me discomfort or sadness, but instead provide insight that life is both joyful and sad simultaneously."

Mark sees this journal as a complex series of interrelated life events, most of which he believes we have little control over. The journal is also a "reminder of how enormously complex our lives are."

Mark shared a final insight about his practice of journal keeping: "The very reason most of us fail to keep a journal is the notion that each entry should be meaningful to all who read it. Most of us typically think of our days as 'routine.' But when they're viewed from a holistic perspective and context (such as a personal journal), I've found it's just not true. Our lives are truly colorful and fascinating in myriad, small ways. Isn't life ironic?"

Dana Fox Jenkins:
The Journal as Crucible

One of the pleasures of writing this book has been discovering the vast range of approaches to journal keeping and the sometimes elaborate and wonderful nuttiness of the styles of journals people keep. Especially fun have been the surprises. For example, I've known Dana Fox Jenkins for several years as a highly energetic yet disciplined and well-organized person. She has a very demanding day job as Assistant VP for Organizational Performance Improvement at a large metropolitan hospital, yet she has managed to sustain a rich and very successful artistic practice. Anyone who can do this must have strong organizational skills, and I reasoned that perhaps her journal practice was the key to keeping it all under control. I expected to see tidy journals, all labeled, numbered, and filed on a set of serious shelves. But I was so wrong! When I told this to Dana, she laughed and said: "I want journals that look like they're a page away from disintegration."

Collecting the Chaos of Daily Life

Dana explained that she's always been a list maker and a "ripper." She has many notebooks in which she jots down lists, passing thoughts, quotes, scraps of fabric, and quick drawings of patterns. "Sometimes I write down words that someone else spoke because I want to remember or riff on them later. I pull out pages from the many magazines I read and I stuff or glue them into journals. The messier, the better. I don't want neat, glued pieces and parts."

Dana was not exaggerating about the messy aspect. Her journals are actually more like crucibles in which unlikely ideas and disparate images ferment alongside each other. For two years, she's been keeping what she calls her "idea" journal to store "everything from random quotes, phone numbers, concepts for special projects—even a few small snippets of ripped pages."

But as soon as one of the concepts grows into a real plan for a piece of art, she starts a separate journal for that project—sort of like removing a seedling from a seedbed and putting it into its own pot.

Currently, she has several project journals in the works. One is tabbed with Post-it notes that say things like "handwritten recipes,"

"ephemera ideas," and "look of the show." The section labeled "frames" is filled with quick drawings of picture frames Dana collected for an upcoming show of her paintings: "I've noted outer and inner dimensions and a likely image size on each. In order to do the show, I need to have a concept in my mind—what it will look like, what might be happening, music, time of year, etc. I put all that in a book."

Another ongoing journal that Dana keeps is a little book for 30-second sketches made while she travels (but not while she's driving, she added) through the mountains. Most of the sketches have quick color notes, and to a few she added watercolor later. Dana uses writing, drawing, painting, and collecting in her journals, although, she says, "I can't say I exactly write, not in many contiguous sentences at least. I mostly write words, phrases, a few complete sentences. Often I haven't a clue what I meant, and sometimes I can't read what I've written."

Dana uses different kinds of books for different kinds of journals, depending on her plan for a given journal and where she is when she decides she needs it. She buys interesting-looking blank books, including many fabric-covered ones. She explained,

"I've often gone away on business and not taken anything to draw with, knowing that I'd be too busy … and of course this makes me compulsively need to draw something. See this little book? It's been in my bag for a year and is now filled. I hope to find another one just like it. I see really interesting books all over the place and I buy them, and the projects seem to find them! I discovered one made from recycled brown paper bags, and each page was a little pocket. The book is probably 5 by 5 inches [12.7 x 12.7 cm]. It turned out to be perfect for a series of paintings I did on the gardens in my neighborhood. I took reference photos of them and put petals in each pocket along with the photo. I used it for a year. It was really helpful, and I still have it, fat and full."

Dana said that she "of course" has travel journals with paintings and notes. "No folder of photos can possibly prompt as much memory as those," she said. She has also kept what I would call practice journals. One year she did a little painting of the weather everyday for a year. Another year she did a different small painting each day.

Setting the Stage to Paint

When I asked Dana what her journals have helped her to do and how they have changed her experiences, she explained that she can't begin an art project without planning, and the journals help her decide "when and where and how," and eventually she's ready to begin:

"I know some painters who work this through on canvas. I do it on paper before I begin painting. If I didn't go through this process, I don't think I'd begin … ever. And, I enjoy the process. It's very creative and energizing … sort of like walking into Pearl Paint in New York and seeing all those boxes of pastels stacked up to the ceilings, or going into a fabulous fabric store … the possibilities are endless at that moment. The reality of doing it hasn't intervened."

Annie Cicale:
Beyond Rules and Forms

Annie Cicale has taught art, calligraphy, and book-arts workshops for many years. She is the author of *The Art and Craft of Hand Lettering* (Lark, 2004). One cold December day, I sat across from Annie at a broad worktable in her studio, on which she had just plunked down an armload of small, well-worn, chunky black books. On a nearby table was a tall stack of handsome, floppy-covered, ledger-style books. Because my own motley collection of journals seems to reflect a mind that cannot settle, I'm intrigued by people who find one or two book forms and stick with them.

Annie has kept a journal of one kind or another since high school, when she started a sketchbook as an art class assignment. She says about her initial approach, "I had seen other sketchbooks and diaries, and felt that mine would have to adhere to the formats, subject matter, and nice handwriting of others' work. Some of that was good in that I learned to write more beautifully and draw carefully. It took me a while, though, to document my own thoughts and ideas, rather than follow the *rules*." In time, she began to include reflections on art shows she had seen, and then to document her thoughts and ideas alongside her sketches.

The Walking Around Books

About 10 years after high school, Annie began to keep what she calls her "walking around books." These are the chunky, little black books, and they reveal the continuing evolution of her artistic practice. The first walking around journal is filled with writing, a complete contrast to her sketchbooks. Over the 30 years that she kept these books, she drew in them more frequently, but now the journals are roughly half writing and half drawing. She works in these little books while waiting for a friend at a restaurant, stuck in traffic, or sitting in an airport. The pages are alive with movie and book titles, notes from workshops and lectures, and sketches of the passing scene. The books reflect her many interests and experiences. For example, one contains sailboat-racing records from when she worked as a buoy keeper.

I watched Annie use one of her walking around books while we were touring a small hill town in Italy. When we stopped to rest, Annie discovered a drain grate in the middle of the path, and began to sketch in her book. The result was a beautiful pen and ink study of the pattern of the grate interrupted by a few stones that were caught in it, like whole notes along a line of sheet music.

New Forms

In addition to the walking around books, Annie keeps other kinds of journals, one of which I would call a "new learning journal." Even though she teaches calligraphy classes and has written one of the definitive books on the subject, she continues to study letterforms. She uses these books to practice traditional letterforms and to invent

but rather than using a photo as a reference for details. I just designed the details to go in the book, repeating motifs, thinking about the overall effect, and making it all relate somehow. The photos will be great as a screen saver memento, but I don't NEED them. I'm sure I knew this before — I seldom use reference photos, but this experience confirmed it for me.

scene from train window. The umbrella trees and the cypress were planted regularly on the path to the old tower.

in San Casciano
Grill with rocks
The gravel was a consistent size, and somewhat rectangular. Some have fallen through, others have lodged themselves in the grid, looking like an abacus.

new forms and alphabets. She designs each page meticulously. These books are large, hand-bound, and reflect the disciplined process of calligraphy. She uses the contents as models for her students to learn from.

Over the years, Annie's family of journals has grown to include travel journals, knitting journals, and color theory exercise journals.

I have a hunch that a person's earliest journal experiences influence later works. Annie's history as a journal-maker suggests this may be true. From the very beginning, her journals have had a consistent internal structure. They're not random collages of haphazard elements, but thoughtful works that are related by harmonious design and attention to detail. Even the casual carry-abouts are all the same size and color, and have a quiet elegance that stems from her calligraphic handwriting and her nuanced studies in pen and ink. Structure seems to free Annie, a former chemical engineer, in the same way that a well-described problem frees the solver to be creative in finding the answer.

Heather Allen-Swarttouw: Filtering Experience

Early in our conversation, artist Heather Allen-Swarttouw described her journals as places where she collects things: they are "filters" of her experiences. Journaling can be like trawling with a fine net, and Heather emphasized that she puts into her books images and ideas that she thinks are interesting "but doesn't know what to do with yet." I love this idea of using the journal process to beach comb, without the narrow focus that comes from knowing what it is exactly that you're looking for.

An Early Start

Heather's father is a life-long journal keeper, and it was his example that she followed. She remembers her father's journals as being more like logbooks, housing factual rather than emotional details. When the family went on camping or sailing trips, her father would read his daily journal entries to them at night. From him Heather got the idea of recording on a daily basis those things that, for some reason or other, caught her interest. Heather's first journal, in second grade, was a spiral-bound, brightly colored book with rounded corners, and in it she recorded her daily observations of the transformation of a caterpillar into a monarch butterfly.

Over the years, Heather continued to keep journals, such as one that she kept while living for a year as a high school exchange student in Japan. Every day her host mother would prepare her lunch box, called an *obento*; the box itself and the arrangement of the food were works of art. Heather painted the contents of her beautiful obento each day.

Heather kept other diaries and journals as she grew up, including a few "therapy journals," her term for notebooks filled with emotional entries. Then, in 1986, Heather's childhood home burned, and all of her journals up to that

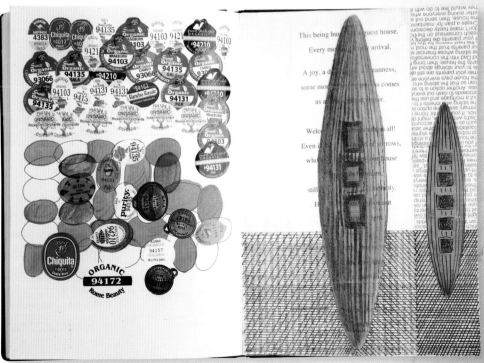

I was particularly interested in Heather's Train Travel journal, one she began on a recent trip to Japan. She was interested in the forms and shapes of the language, so she began collecting samples of Japanese writing that focused on the pattern of the writing.

Heather also keeps a gardening journal, a ceramics ideas journal, and a poetry journal. In all of these she collects ideas by sketching, writing, drawing, and pasting in things.

date were lost in the fire. When I expressed dismay, Heather said she actually found it "very freeing," so much so that not too many years ago she intentionally burned all of her "therapy journals." She described the process: "The black ink spread to the paper as it burned, turning the paper black. Then suddenly it all turned to white ash and was gone." All of the angst and introspection vanished with the ash. She would never, she emphasized, burn one of her other kinds of journals—those in which she collects images and ideas. She returns to them for inspiration, to get ideas of where her artwork is going.

These days Heather enjoys using her Won't Leave Home Without It journal, which she carries with her everywhere. Everything goes into these slim black leather books that seems in any way interesting. She combines writing, drawing, and painting, as well as a little collage. Each book covers a single year.

Heather is also working in more than a dozen other journals. There is her Swatch Book, a stab-bound soft-covered journal that contains swatches of all the different fabrics she has created. She's named another book her Snowstorm Journal. She made this book with black pages, and she began drawing and writing in it during, of course, a snowstorm. The sketches and passages of writing done in white pencil or pen on the black paper mirror the white and black world of a snowstorm and play tricks with perception and vision, introducing a new way of looking at things.

I was drawn to one very different-looking journal in the pile of books: it had a furry white rabbit skin cover that softly flopped over the text block. Heather explained that this is her birthday journal, with the cover chosen especially for her, because she was born in the year of the rabbit in the Chinese calendar. She uses this journal each year to write reflections on her birthday.

Using the Journals

Although Heather considers all of her journals to be filters of some kind, she has one journal that she calls her Filter Journal. Its pages show photocopied images and written entries from her everyday journals. In this book she brings together related images and ideas that she has collected at different times. She cross-pollinates images in this way, and sometimes reworks them. This journal seems to me to be a step further in the direction of using the journal as a source for creative expression.

In Heather's garden journal there are several pages devoted to careful drawings of seedpods, others to flowers and other plant parts, including seeds. In one of her sculptures, you can see traces of the pod form that she abstracted and joined with several spherical forms that echoed some of the seed drawings. Heather had combined and refined nascent and disparate images and ideas, safely stored in her journal, to create a beautiful piece of artwork.

Sandy Webster: Documentation

Sandy Webster creates artists' books, paintings, prints, sculpture, and drawings. A few minutes into our conversation about her journal practice, I asked her what she remembered as her first journal-keeping experience.

"How do you define a journal?" she responded. Sandy considers a true journal to be a book that one keeps for oneself—uncensored, unedited, and never shown to other people. She considers the relatively new art journals that have proliferated to be a different kind of expression, because the intention to make them public changes the way the keeper of the book works. I share her viewpoint.

Sandy has always recorded her experiences in a notebook using both writing and drawing. Keeping a journal is a process for Sandy, not a result: "I have a deep need to document my life experiences. The entries create a path back to the emotional content of an experience. It's so delicious to walk back into that day, I can look at a small line drawing of a ferry crossing to Whidbey Island and I can taste the mussels and hear people talking at the pub on the island."

Beginnings

The earliest notebooks that Sandy remembers keeping were botanical sketchbooks she drew in when she lived in Michigan in the 1980s. To learn about the wildflowers growing near her house, she began to make detailed colored drawings of each flower. Like the journals she has kept since, these books were done just for her.

Sandy showed me dozens of her books. There are the everyday journals that she carries everywhere, small enough to slide easily in and out of her purse or pocket. She jots down notes and quick sketches describing the passing scene. Sandy also writes down planning lists, book and movie titles, names and phone numbers, words she wants to remember, and ideas she wants to keep in a safe place. One journal I especially loved was her Airplane Fear Journal—a slightly worn little black book that she writes in while sitting in an airport or on the plane. She documents things such as the time of arrival and departure, the gate number, the weather, the skittering and lurching noises of the plane—she calls it her personal Black Box. The journal takes her mind off of flying, and keeps her calm and focused.

Travel Journals

Sandy's travel journals serve several purposes. She makes books (and sometimes boxes for the books) to house her entries long before she leaves on the trip so that the blank journals become a part of the gathering of energy and excitement that help her get ready for an adventure. The travel journals are highly illustrative and document with precise detail everything she notices. Many of them include samples of local soils and paint that she has made using local clay pigments. One noteworthy journal is housed in a box that Sandy prepared by stocking it with very small containers and a minuscule glass vial filled with gum Arabic for making watercolor paint. As she traveled around Australia, she filled the little containers with pigments extracted from the various clays she found there. She then painted the journal using the paints she had made.

This particular journal is easy to mistake for a designed book, a finished product, but Sandy insists it's nothing of the kind. By the time she worked in this journal, she was so practiced in daily drawing and note-taking that the enormous beauty of the pages happened spontaneously. After the Australia trip, Sandy went back to this journal and harvested images and ideas from its pages to serve as the basis of later artwork. The journal itself remains a personal documentation and exploration.

Another kind of journal Sandy keeps is her teaching and learning books. These are samplers, comprised of all the techniques and processes she teaches in a particular workshop. Sandy keeps many other unique journals, such as one devoted to sketches of her cats, another with her drawings done while visiting museums, and one about her garden.

A final and remarkable journal is the project book about building her house. When Sandy and her husband set out to build a house, she immediately made a book to—what else?—document the process. The hard board cover is encrusted with soil from the land, and the book itself is solid, heavy, and fits the hand like a brick or a short length of 2-by-6. Inside is a wealth of information: the price of everything from nails and insulation to the cost of labor to dig the foundation and lay the stones; drawings of all the workmen and building tools; sketches of the site before the house was built; drawings of the newly-planted trees and shrubbery; notes about delays in materials delivery; excited commentary about the project's progress. The last page has a cut-through, a doorway through which Sandy drew the back of the moving van as it departed on moving day.

I asked Sandy if she had any favorites amongst her many books. She said, "No, whatever is necessary is what I do. I'm rarely concerned about it as a product. I just want it to be useful, accessible, and document my experiences."

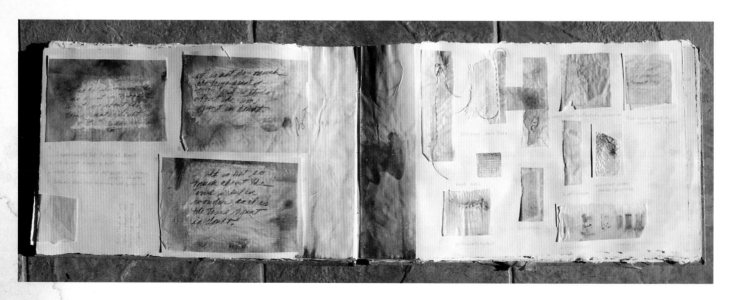

MARGARET COGSWELL
Journal Book #4, 2008
4⅝ x 4⅝ inches
(11.8 x 11.8 cm); gouache,
graphite, paper scraps,
marker, ink, shellac

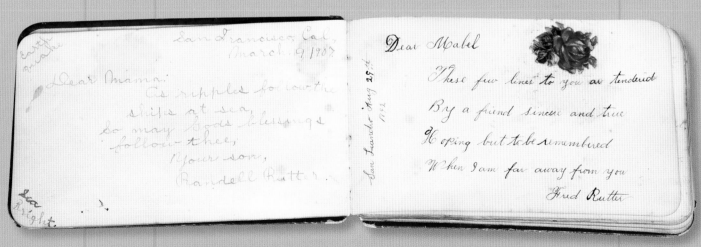

MABEL FOSSETTE RUTTER   *Autograph Book,* 1890–1915
7¾ x 4¾ (19.7 x 12 cm); courtesy of Kristine Vogdes

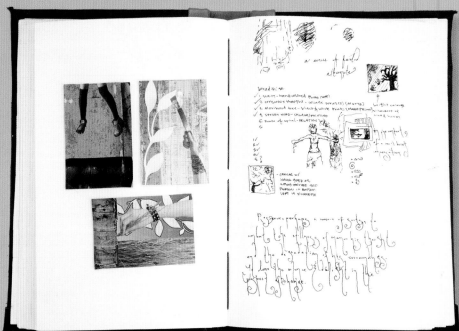

LEILA SCOGIN
Doodlebook, **2008**
3½ x 5½ inches (8.9 x 14 cm);
leather, fabric; ink, paper collage

ELIZABETH ELLISON *Deep Creek in May*
page in *May 02 '02–March 27 '03,* **2003**
12½ x 12½ inches (31.8 x 31.8 cm); color-sketched
purchased journal book; watercolor, ink

GWEN DIEHN *Women's Artistic*
Vision Class Group Notebook, **1997**
9 x 12 x 2 (22.9 x 30.5 x 5.1 cm); hand-bound
book by David Diehn; pen acrylic, pencil

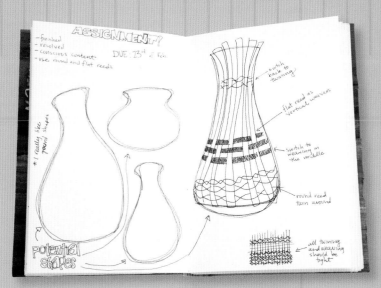

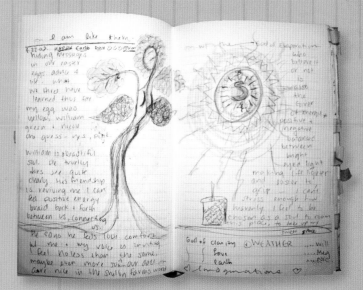

MARY VAN EGMOND *New Learning Journal*, 2009
6 x 7 inches (15.2 x 17.8 cm); pencil, pen

MEGAN STONE *Imaginations*, 2003
9½ x 12 inches (24.1 x 30.5 cm); colored pencil, ink PHOTO BY ARTIST

JESSICA HERMAN GOODSON
Unbroken Wings, 2009
8¾ x 14 x 1½ inches
(22.2 x 35.6 x 3.8 cm);
collage, paint, pen, pencil
PHOTO BY ARTIST

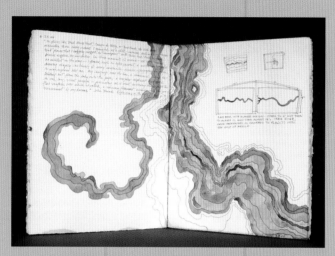

JULIE WAGNER *Working Journal for The Littoral Zone,* **2004–2009**
15 x 11½ x ¾ inches (38.1 x 29.2 x 1.9 cm); handmade book, ink
and watercolor on Rives BFK Moulin de Güe PHOTO BY ARTIST
Quote from Reflections in the Lizard's Eye by John Brandi;
Western Edge Press, 2000 USED WITH PERMISSION

LOY McWHIRTER *the womynne withe deamonnes*
poemme, illuminated somewhatte forre one of the
daemonnes inne honourre of his thirty-third birthdaye, **1984**
9 x 6 inches (22.9 x 15.2 cm); brown construction paper cover,
sketchbook paper, sewing thread, rapidograph pen, ink
PHOTO BY BRUCE GREENE

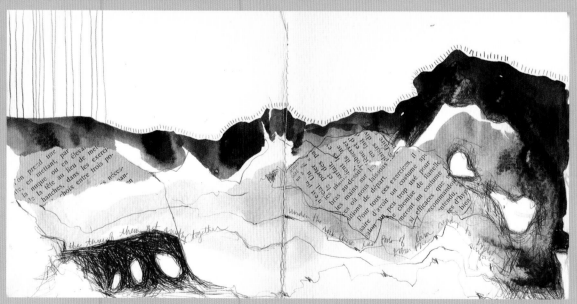

TARA CHICKEY
Untitled, 2008
5 x 10 inches
(12.7 x 25.4 cm);
handmade book;
ink, pencil,
collage, watercolor
PHOTO BY ARTIST

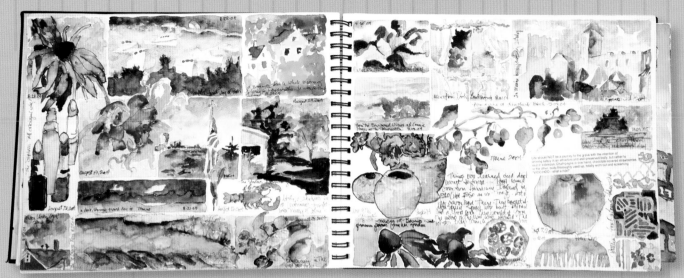

DANA FOX JENKINS *Painting-a-Day Journal*, 2005
12 x 16 inches (30.5 x 40.6 cm); pencil, watercolors, collage

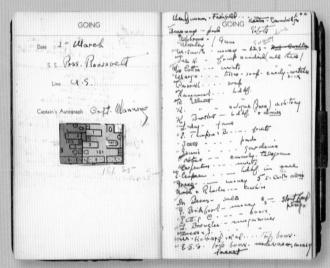

AGNES MORTON SHAW *Personal travel notes (re: name of ship and captain, insert of layout of cabin, and list of gifts purchased) made in purchased travel diary*, 1939
Ellen Eddy Shaw Papers, Special Collections, Brooklyn Botanic Garden Library

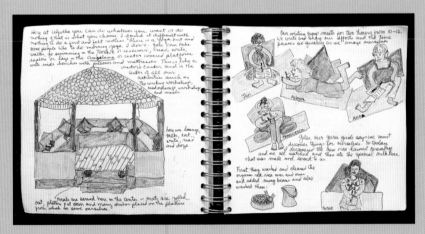

JAN WHEATCROFT *Sri Lanka; Ambalamba*, 2000
7 x 5 inches (17.8 x 12.7 cm); pen, watercolors PHOTO BY GENARO MOLINA

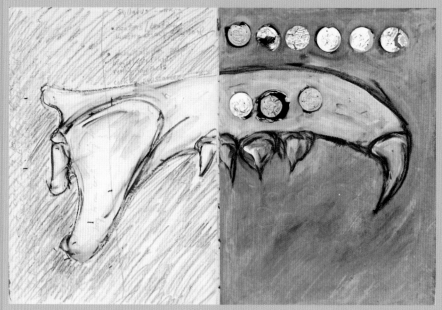

ANDREA PETERSON
Glowlab Sketchbook 5, 2009
12 x 18 inches (30.5 x 45.7 cm);
goache, pencil, wine tops PHOTO BY ARTIST

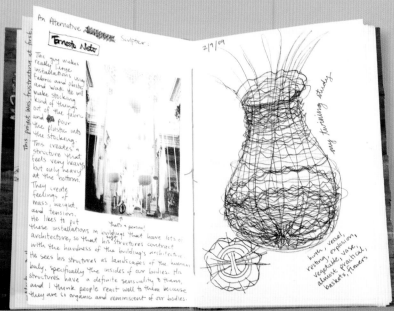

MARY VAN EGMOND *New Learning Journal*, 2009
6 x 7 inches (15.2 x 17.8 cm); pencil, pen

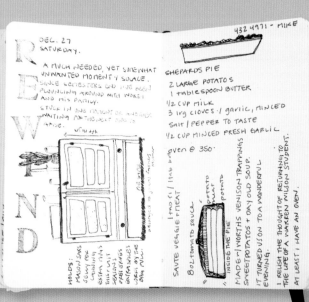

LIZ PULLAN *Foods Journal*, 2008–2009
3½ x 5 inches (8.9 x 12.7 cm); pen

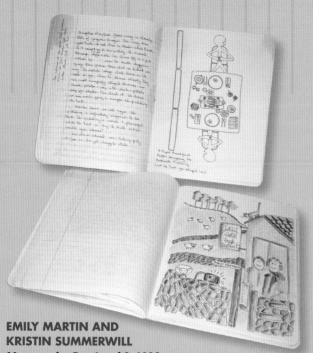

**EMILY MARTIN AND
KRISTIN SUMMERWILL**
Money and a Car, 1 and 2, **1996**
Modified composition book; pen, colored pencils
PHOTO BY ARTIST—Emily and Kristin both worked in
these two journals on a trip to London, swapping
them back and forth after each daily entry.

SARAH A. BOURNE *Daily Journal Page,* **2009**
5 x 7 inches (12.7 x 17.8 cm); store-bought journal;
watercolor, ink PHOTO BY ARTIST

BRUCE KREMER
9–10July93, **1993**
8 x 11 inches (20.3 x 27.9 cm);
combined materials in a diary

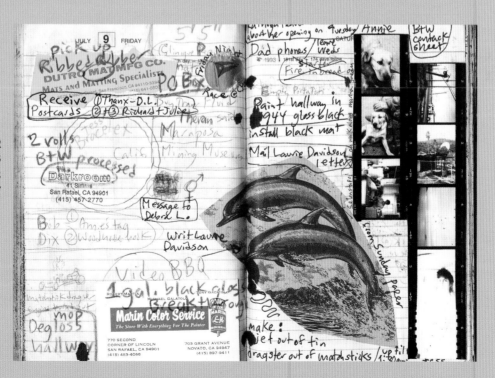

Acknowledgments

One of the greatest pleasures of writing this book has been the opportunity to collaborate with people whose interesting and unpredictable journal practices far surpassed anything I could have imagined when I started. I have been amazed by the generosity of the journal keepers, who not only tested my initial efforts at the *Choose Your Own Bookbinding Adventure* booklet, but went on to keep their self-designed journals for several months, trusting me when I suggested this journal project might actually be worth their time: Brigid Burns, Rebecca Blass-Casey, Chris Kobler, Fran Loges, Jane Hale McSpadden, Micah and Rob Pulleyn, Ann Turkle, and Mary Daugherty and her five grandsons.

For their gift of time and for sharing their talents, I thank the long-time journal keepers who opened their studios to me when it was possible, and when it was not, shipped boxes and boxes of journals to me, trusting the post office and me to return them: Annie Cicale, Mark Combs, Dana Fox Jenkins, Heather Allen-Swarttouw, and Sandy Webster. A special thanks to Gisela Probst, who told me as much as she remembered about Otto Probst's journal practice, and then carefully boxed up a number of his journals and shipped them to me.

I owe the clarity and completeness of the bookbinding instructions to the Warren Wilson College students in my Bookforms I and II classes in Fall 2008. They field-tested the *Choose Your Own Bookbinding Adventure* booklet, used the written instructions to make their class notebooks, and gave me excellent feedback for improving the directions in this book: Azzizi Ahdoot, Georgia Anton, Emma Berger-Singer, Grace Crowley, Chelsea Gay, Paige Heron, Geneva Isaacs, Cameron Lash, Jillian Levy, Julia Mead, Jacob Salt, Alexandra Uchniat, Mary Allene VanEgmond, and Kate Ziegler. I want to give special thanks to Kerstin Vogdes, my daughter-in-law, who field-tested instructions and kept a travel journal; who always gives me incisive, honest, and eminently useful feedback; and who cheerfully bails me out of all my computer problems.

Researching the sidebars was one of my favorite parts of writing the book. I thank Kathy Crosby, librarian at the Brooklyn Botanic Garden Library, for not only letting me camp out there one long summer afternoon, but for sharing treasures from the collection that she thought might interest me. I also thank Charles Ritchie, Associate

GWEN DIEHN *Palazzone Wedding Planning Journal,* **2005**
5 x 7 x 1 inches (12.7 x 17.8 x 2.5 cm); watercolor, gouache, acrylic absorbent ground, pen, rubber stamp letters on handmade paper

Curator in the Department of Modern Prints and Drawings at the National Gallery of Art in Washington, D.C., who kindly showed me his favorites from the collection and arranged for my use of the image from the Oscar Bluemner sketchbook, a journal that I would have not known about without his help. Thanks are also due to Paul Huth and Shanan Smiley of the Daniel Smiley Research Center of the Mohonk Preserve for their generous support.

There could not have been a better group of people to shepherd a manuscript from scribbles on the backs of envelopes to a finished product than the team at Lark Books: Deborah Morgenthal, my editor; Dana Irwin, the art director; Shannon Yokeley, Dana's assistant; Celia Naranjo, the cover designer; and Mark Bloom and Beth Sweet, assistant editors and tireless researchers. Deborah, especially, championed the book from its beginning and was my friend and ally while keeping me realistic. She and Dana were wonderfully flexible and creative about finding ways to do the design things I wanted to do within budgetary limits. Proofreaders Jessica Boing and Kate Mathews found and fixed the loose ends, and I thank them too.

Finally, thanks to all of the journal keepers who let us photograph their journals. The richness and diversity of their pages are at the heart of this book.

About the Author

Gwen Diehn's prints, drawings, and artists' books have been exhibited widely and are in many collections, including The National Museum of Women in the Arts, Washington, DC. She has taught drawing, printmaking, artists' books, and watercolor for many years. She is the author of several other Lark books, including *The Complete Decorated Journal* (2012).

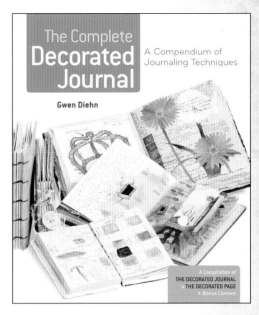

Now two of Gwen Diehn's most successful books, *The Decorated Page* and *The Decorated Journal*, are bound together in this comprehensive and inspiring volume that teaches readers how to create both engaging journals and journal pages. Gwen explores a variety of easy-to-use materials and offers an unmatched collection of great ideas and techniques, from innovative layouts to simple bookbindings.

Contributors Index

Index